MW01463511

ON! THE FUTURE OF NOW
Making Sense of our Always On, Always Connected World

Curated by Toby Daniels and Craig Hepburn

Edited by Caroline McCarthy

Published by Crowdcentric Media in partnership with
Social Media Week and Nokia

Copyright © 2014 Crowdcentric Media.

All rights reserved. No part of this book may be reproduced, stored, or transmitted by any means—whether auditory, graphic, mechanical, or electronic—without written permission of both publisher and author, except in the case of brief excerpts used in critical articles and reviews. Unauthorized reproduction of any part of this work is illegal and is punishable by law.

ISBN: 978-1-4834-1242-9 (sc)
ISBN: 978-1-4834-1241-2 (e)

Library of Congress Control Number: 2014909092

Because of the dynamic nature of the Internet, any web addresses or links contained in this book may have changed since publication and may no longer be valid. The views expressed in this work are solely those of the author and do not necessarily reflect the views of the publisher, and the publisher hereby disclaims any responsibility for them.

Any people depicted in stock imagery provided by Thinkstock are models, and such images are being used for illustrative purposes only. Certain stock imagery © Thinkstock.

Lulu Publishing Services rev. date: 5/16/2014

Contents

Foreword by Scott Harrison 2
Preface by Toby Daniels and Craig Hepburn 5

PART 1: When Humans and Technology Unite 12
1. This is the new "now." 12
2. What Nobody's Talking About 18
3. Beyond the Human Being Operating System 24
4. Stay Human 30
5. Games in the Gheralta 34
6. Neighbors 38

PART 2: The Fight for Our Attention 42
7. Surviving the Bankruptcy of Our Attention 42
8. The Daily You 46
9. If Cats Could Play Miley Cyrus 52
10. Trapped by TL;DR 60

PART 3: Innovating With the User in Mind 64
11. Getting Past the Long, Dark Scandinavian Winter 64
12. Trust Through Anonymity: A Look At The Chinese Internet 70
13. If It Will Work In Africa, It Will Work Anywhere 74
14. When Handwriting Recognition Saves Lives 80
15. Culturability 84
16. Antuyo 90

PART 4: Changing the World Through Technology 94
17. Transforming Sport, Transforming Society 94
18. How to Save Marketing 98
19. Knowledge Is The New Land 106
20. The Collaborative Economy 110

A Summary 116
Acknowledgements 117
About Social Media Week 118
About Crowdcentric Media 118
About the Curators 119

Foreword by Scott Harrison

founder, charity:water

A couple of years ago, entrepreneur and philanthropist Michael Birch said to me, "You're surprisingly bad at technology."

Most people thought we — and by "we" I mean charity:water, the nonprofit organization I founded in order to bring clean and safe drinking water to everyone on the planet — were pretty good with technology. We were the first nonprofit to hit a million followers on Twitter. We have our own fundraising platform where people have generously raised money for us by "giving up" their birthdays and soliciting donations from family and friends. But in reality, I think what we were good at in charity:water's first few years was storytelling and design, not technology. We focused a lot on the brand — on hope, and possibility, and telling these inspirational stories as opposed to some of the guilt- and shame-based "poverty porn" that people had gotten used to.

Michael Birch, best known for founding the social network Bebo, helped us build our first fundraising platform, but nothing was really being measured or instrumented until early 2013. I was in Ethiopia with Greg Pass, the former CTO of Twitter who's now the Chief Entrepreneurial Officer of the Cornell tech campus in New York, and in the back of a Land Rover he told me about instrumentation. It's kind of embarrassing, but I couldn't believe just how much I didn't know about how our website behaves and how our users are behaving. When I got back to New York, I immediately put more focus on engineering and product development, and the things we started to learn — understanding every side of our technology and realizing the kinds of new possibilities we could unlock — were amazing.

The fact of the matter is, it's an incredible time to live in a world where we are constantly connected and able to communicate across borders and languages and cultures. Having a million Twitter followers is just scratching the surface … what's become possible through digital innovation is truly incredible, and that's what you're going to read about in the essays in this book.

In the nonprofit world, the bar has historically been set very low for digital innovation. One of the things that perplexes me the most is direct mail — it must work to some degree, because people keep doing it, but no one I know is writing checks to these charities through mailbox solicitations. Maybe it's working for a demographic that's aging, but I write one check a month for my rent in NYC and the minute I don't have to write that check I'm going to throw out my checkbook. I interact with almost the entire world online and certainly the people I know that are younger, certainly the teenagers today, are not writing checks.

We're just early adopters. We have a very young culture at the office. The minute Twitter came out we got charity:water an account. Same with Instagram and Pinterest. We're not married or loyal to any product or technology, we just better be trying them all out. A traditional charity might wait for two or three years, watch something like Twitter and then decide they need to figure out a Twitter strategy, and then go hire someone to manage their social media … and then they're a few years late.

Constant connectivity, rapid change, and innovation on all fronts — that's "the future of now." And at charity:water we're excited by how that can change lives. It's already been a big part of charity:water's brand and loyalty that all of the wells we dig, now in 20 different countries, can be tracked on Google Earth. Now, going a step further, we're really excited about the project that we've been working on thanks to a $5 million grant from the Google Impact Awards to go and develop a remote sensor that we could put in our rural water projects that would let us know back here in New York how much water was flowing from each well. We've had 10 labs working on it. We're making tons of progress, but it's been challenging, and we finally now think we have a sensor that's going to work well for a test run.

And that would be game changing — I could turn on a smartphone and show you how much water flowed today from a well that you helped sponsor in rural Ethiopia. The transparency there, the kind of connective tissue that a relatively affordable device could provide could be really important to our business. We'd be showing people that the money is having an impact and that people are being served and that water is flowing.

I want to personally thank you for supporting charity:water with your purchase of this book. We couldn't be more thrilled about what's happening now, and what's next ... and, increasingly, these two time frames seem closer to each other than ever. The curiosity of people like you about the global changes we face as we become increasingly connected will fuel the exchange of ideas that have put us on a path to solving massive problems like the availability of clean water around the world.

"Let's keep the water - and ideas - flowing."

Scott Harrison, Founder and CEO, charity: water

In 2004, Scott served as a photojournalist for Mercy Ships in Liberia, West Africa, where he learned about the life-threatening effects of contaminated water. Upon moving back home to New York City in 2006 he founded charity: water.

Learn more about Scott Harrison at www.charitywater.org.

Preface by Toby Daniels and Craig Hepburn

If you worked in tech and lived in America in 2008, you witnessed what I witnessed — the transformative power of social media. An entire nation of optimistic and passionate young people came together to take action for something they believed in: to get behind and elect a president who would represent them in the fight for political, social, and economic change. The engine of this movement was the will of the people, but the fuel was the self-organizing capability of social media.

The communications revolution, as it has become known, had been building for years prior to 2008, but it was not until a critical mass of people became connected to each other through social networks such as Facebook and Twitter and through smartphone devices that we realized the extent to which it would impact our lives; not just here in the U.S., but globally. When you connect the world through open networks, in a frictionless way and across cultural, economic, and geographic boundaries the possibilities are limitless in terms of what we might be able to achieve. Access to more information, leads to better education and as we know, education is the source of economic prosperity.

So, in 2008, and faced with the significance of what was unfolding, I asked myself — what role did I want to play? I'm a Brit who had moved to the States in 2006 and had recently left a startup — so how did I want to contribute to the next communication revolution? Did I want to start a new company? Did I want to do something in the social impact space and do something more centrally focused on solving societal problems? Or did I want to get back into the world of tech and interactive media?

In 2008 I didn't really have the answers to these questions; everything felt so nascent and so fragmented, but I knew I wanted to surround myself with people who were as fascinated about what was happening in social media as I was. The trouble was that when I looked around at conferences I was attending and speaking at, I was concerned that few people were tackling the tough questions and looking at was happening through the same lens as me and a handful of my peers.

To me, social media was *the* new communications paradigm that not only needed to be understood, but also explored and experimented with. So I started Social Media Week — a living and breathing example of a collaborative and decentralized attempt at convening people with the aim of creating new ways for us to understand how to move forward and to advance our understanding of what was happening and what might be next.

It began as an experiment in trying to elevate the conversation by having the smartest people across a range of diverse areas of expertise curate the content. Since then, it has evolved into a platform that has expanded to 18 countries, across five continents, which reaches hundreds of thousands of people through localized events and millions more through social, mobile, and online. Our ambition has always been to reach and impact as many people as possible — which is still our goal today — so expanding internationally was fairly straightforward for us, because we designed the model to function in a distributed and decentralized way with local partners handling all the operational aspects of running the conference.

Getting to this point has required a level of collaboration and cooperation that I have could never have imagined possible, and something I could not have conceived of when we started out. But by 2011, we clearly needed a global partner in addition to our regional partners — one that shared our affinity for discussing the intersection of technology and humanity. So when we thought about a suitable partner we asked ourselves, which global brands embody a similar mission? My first and only thought was Nokia. This is a company with which I had a deep, nostalgic relationship. My first phone was a Nokia and their "Connecting People" slogan had always felt so strong and enduring. Admittedly, in 2011 this was a company going through some major challenges. However, I was convinced that they would be an incredible collaborator given their size, global footprint and corporate values.

After a few second- and third-degree connections from friends in the summer of 2010, I met Craig Hepburn and, following a number of exploratory conversations, Nokia became Social Media Week's Global Headline sponsor in 2011. At that time, we had expanded to 11 cities globally and were bringing together around 20,000 attendees across all the conferences we were hosting. Since then, and with Craig's vision and Nokia's support, we have expanded to more than 26 cities, and hosted conferences in cities like Bogota, Colombia; Lagos, Nigeria; Mumbai; and Copenhagen. In 2014, we will add Bangalore, Sydney and Johannesburg to the mix.

The journey over the past five years has been one of discovery and exploration into how different cultures around the world are embracing social media and mobile technology to advance themselves economically, socially, and culturally. The journey would not have been possible without Nokia's support, and the decision to write this book is partly a way to celebrate what we have accomplished together.

Partway through 2013, Craig and I were meeting in London to discuss plans for SMW and Nokia's partnership in 2014, and he suggested we write a book to tell the story of the past four years. At the time I laughed off the idea, partly because writing a book intimidated the hell out of me, and partly because I didn't think people would care that much about what we had to say.

But then I thought, what if we approached writing the book in the same way we approach building SMW? Rather than our voices being the strongest, and, rather than us dictating the content, what if we crowdsourced contributions from people who share our passion but who offered unique perspectives? What if some of those people included Seth Godin, Douglas Rushkoff, Cindy Gallop, Robin Chase, and Jonah Peretti? And what if we donated the proceeds from the sale of the book to an incredible nonprofit organization like charity:water?

And so the book was born.

On! The Future of Now, is released to you in beta version, which means we're just at the beginning of our journey towards our mission. It represents collaboration and co-creation and, through a collection of incredible essays by some brilliant people, tells a story of how our lives are being shaped by social media and how our relationship to technology and to one other is evolving. The contents of this book are both powerful and inspiring and, above all, thought provoking. We hope you enjoy it, and we thank you for supporting us and charity:water by purchasing it.

- Toby Daniels

In 2010, shortly after I had joined Nokia as global director of digital and social media, I was introduced by our head of brand to an Englishman in New York. I was really trying to find a purpose, vision, and cause that would support the Nokia vision to "connect people" while also providing a vehicle for thought leadership and product advocacy. As it turns out, that Englishman in New York was Toby Daniels, who was at the time looking to secure a global partner for Social Media Week. Toby and his team really had a strong vision of what type of brand and company they wanted to work with; for them, it was important to find a brand with a common vision for technology, social media, and the impact on society and culture. After many extensive meetings between both our teams and companies, it became increasingly apparent that there was a powerful shared vision we could work with.

Over the years, through the ensuing Social Media Week and Nokia's partnership, we have been able to help drive change within our organization and provide a vehicle for our employees to showcase incredible digital work, engage in more meaningful ways with our advocates, build better relationships with consumers and even actively turn rejecters of the Nokia brand into fans of our products and services. For me, Social Media Week was not just "another" social media or digital event; it was a movement that had a cause at the center of its purpose: to help people unlock the hot debates around technology and social media in today's society. But Social Media Week also is helping people better understand the culture of technological change that has become overloaded with information — news feeds, tweets, Facebook posts, YouTube videos, Vines, Instagram photos, SMS, emails, ads through our TVs, mobiles, tablets, phablets, and all other types of connected technology we all interface with on a regular basis.

One of the most exciting and valuable outcomes of our partnership with SMW over the years has been the opportunity to engage our local markets in the events that happen twice per year — once in February and again in September — when we enable the local Nokia teams to get deeply involved in cultural debates on the use of mobile and social media in their cities, build new advocacy relationships and showcase the incredible work and innovation of Nokia products and services. This creates a powerful platform for Nokia to participate in the debate around technological, mobile and digital shifts happening across our world today. As a mobile and services company, it's never been more important to be part of the debate and also to have a strong point of view on the impact of digital technology in today's society.

Now in our fourth year, we at Nokia are very proud to be the global partner of Social Media Week and have never been more excited to be part of the debate on "The Future of Now" exploring how technology, social media and mobile are impacting society, culture, and business. Never in human history have we had to deal with so much change at the pace at which it is happening. The growth of social media, along with both mobile content consumption and creation, means that we are constantly at risk of content and data overload.

One of my favorite quotations from Charlie Chaplin comes from "The Great Dictator":

> "We have developed speed, but we have shut ourselves in. Machinery that gives abundance has left us in want. Our knowledge has made us cynical. Our cleverness, hard and unkind. We think too much and feel too little. More than machinery we need humanity. More than cleverness we need kindness and gentleness. Without these qualities, life will be violent and all will be lost …"

So the questions we now need to be asking and dealing with as a society are how do we cope, manage and make sense of all this content and data, how do we filter the noise, embrace the important stuff and take back control of our lives and let technology help us in work, family, and business? How do we embrace all this incredible content and opportunity to connect with the world more often, yet maintain a sense of purpose, emotion and presence?

I highly encourage you to read this book with an open mind, embrace the ideas, argue and debate the thinking being discussed and join the debate online through the hashtag #TheFutureOfNow and at www.socialmediaweek.org.

- Craig Hepburn

PART 1
When Humans and Technology Unite

Chapter 1:

This is the new "now."

By Douglas Rushkoff, author, "Present Shock"

This is adapted from an excerpt of Douglas Rushkoff's book "Present Shock," published in 2013 by Penguin Group.

This is the new "now."

Our society has reoriented itself to the present moment. Everything is live, real time, and always-on. It's not a mere speeding up, however much our lifestyles and technologies have accelerated the rate at which we attempt to do things. It's more of a diminishment of anything that isn't happening right now — and the onslaught of everything that supposedly is.

It's why the world's leading search engine is evolving into a live, customized, and predictive flow of data branded "Google Now;" why email is giving way to texting, and why blogs are being superseded by Twitter feeds. It's why kids in school can no longer follow linear arguments; why narrative structure collapsed into reality TV; and why we can't engage in meaningful dialogue about last month's books and music, much less long-term global issues. It's why an economy once based on long-term investment and interest- bearing currency can no longer provide capital to those who plan to put it to work for future rewards. It's why so many long for a "singularity" or a 2012 apocalypse to end linear time altogether and throw us into a posthistoric eternal present — no matter the cost to human agency or civilization itself.

But it's also how we find out what's happening on the streets of Iran before CNN can assemble a camera crew. It's what enables an unsatisfied but upwardly mobile executive to quit his job and move with his family to Vermont to make kayaks — which he thought he'd get to do only once he retired. It's how millions of young people can choose to embody a new activism based in patient consensus instead of contentious debate. It's what enables companies like H&M or Zara to fabricate clothes in real time, based on the instantaneous data coming from scanned tags at checkout counters five thousand miles away. It's how a president can run for office and win by breaking from the seeming tyranny of the past and its false hope, and tell voters that "we are the ones we have been waiting for."

Well, the waiting is over. Here we are.

If the end of the 20th century can be characterized by futurism, the 21st can be defined by presentism.

The looking forward so prevalent in the late 1990s was bound to end once the new millennium began. Like some others of that era, I predicted a new focus on the moment, on real experience, and on what things are actually worth right now. Then, 9/11 magnified this sensibility, forcing America as a nation to contend with its own impermanence. People had babies in droves, and even filed for divorce, in what was at least an unconscious awareness that none of us lives forever and an accompanying reluctance to postpone things indefinitely. Add real-time technologies, from the iPhone to Twitter; a disposable consumer economy where 1-Click ordering is more important than the actual product being purchased; a multitasking brain actually incapable of storage or sustained argument; and an economy based on spending now what one may or may not earn in a lifetime, and you can't help but become temporally disoriented. It's akin to the onslaught of changing rules and circumstances that 1970's futurist Alvin Toffler dubbed "future shock."

Only, in our era it's more of a present shock. And while this phenomenon is clearly "of the moment," it's not quite as in the moment as we may have expected.

For although many of us were correct about the way all this presentism would affect investments and finance, even technology and media, we were utterly wrong about how living in the "now" would end up impacting us as people. Our focus on the present may have liberated us from the twentieth century's dangerously compelling ideological narratives. No one — well, hardly anyone — can still be convinced that brutal means are justified by mythological ends. And people are less likely to believe employers' and corporations' false promises of future rewards for years of loyalty now. But it has not actually brought us into greater awareness of what is going on around us. We are not approaching some Zen state of an infinite moment, completely at one with our surroundings, connected to others and aware of ourselves on any fundamental level.

Rather, we tend to exist in a distracted present, where forces on the periphery are magnified and those immediately before us are ignored. Our ability to create a plan — much less follow through on it — is undermined by our need to be able to improvise our way through any number of external impacts that stand to derail us at any moment. Instead of finding a stable foothold in the here and now, we end up reacting to the ever-present assault of simultaneous impulses and commands.

In some senses, this was the goal of those who developed the computers and networks on which we depend today. Mid-20th century computing visionaries Vannevar Bush and J. C. R. Licklider dreamed of developing machines that could do our remembering for us. Computers would free us from the tyranny of the past — as well as the horrors of World War II — allowing us to forget everything and devote our minds to solving the problems of today. The information would still be there; it would simply be stored out of body, in a machine.

It's a tribute to both their designs on the future and their devotion to the past that they succeeded in their quest to free up the present of the burden of memory. We have, in a sense, been allowed to dedicate much more of our cognitive resources to active RAM than to maintaining our cerebral-storage hard drives. But we are also in danger of squandering this cognitive surplus on the trivial pursuit of the immediately relevant over any continuance of the innovation that got us to this point.

Behavioral economists exploit the growing disparity between our understanding of the present and that of the future, helping us see future debts as less relevant than current costs and leading us to make financial decisions against our own better interests. As these ways of understanding debt and lending trickle up to those making decisions about banking and macrofinance — such as the Federal Reserve or the European Central Bank — our greater economies end up suffering from the same sorts of logical traps as those of individual mortgage holders and credit card users.

Neuroscientists, mostly at the service of corporations looking to develop more compliant employees and consumers, are homing in on the way people make choices. But no matter how many subjects they put in their MRI machines, the focus of this research is decision-making in the moment, the impulsive choices made in the blink of an eye, rather than those made by the lobes responsible for rational thought or consideration. By implementing their wares solely on the impulsive — while diminishing or altogether disregarding the considered — they push us toward acting in what is thought of as an instinctual, reptilian fashion.

And this mode of behavior is then justified as somehow more connected to the organic, emotional and immediately relevant moment in which human beings actually live. Of course, this depiction of consciousness may help sell the services of neurotechnicians to advertisers, but it does not accurately represent how the human brain relates to the moment in which the organism exists.

No matter how invasive the technologies at their disposal, marketers and pollsters never come to terms with the living process through which people choose products or candidates; they are looking at what people just bought or thought, and making calculations based on that after-the-fact data. The "now" they seek to understand tells them nothing about desire, reasons, or context. It is simply an effort to key off what we have just done in order to manipulate our decisions in the future. Their campaigns encourage the kinds of impulsive behavior that fool us into thinking we are living in the now while actually just making us better targets for their techniques.

That is because there is no now — not the one they're talking about, anyway. It is necessarily and essentially trivial. The minute the "now" is apprehended, it has already passed. Like they used to say about getting one's picture on a Time magazine cover: The moment something is realized, it is over. And like the diminishing beauty returns for a facially paralyzed Botox addict, the more forcefully we attempt to stop the passage of time, the less available we are to the very moment we seek to preserve.

As a result, our culture becomes an entropic, static hum of everybody trying to capture the slipping moment. Narrativity and goals are surrendered to a skewed notion of the real and the immediate; the Tweet; the status update. What we are doing at any given moment becomes all-important — which is behavioristically doomed. For this desperate approach to time is at once flawed and narcissistic. Which "now" is important: the now I just lived or the now I'm in right now?

We need to consider what we human beings can do to pace ourselves and our expectations when there's no temporal backdrop against which to measure our progress, no narrative through which to make sense of our actions, no future toward which we may strive, and seemingly no time to figure any of this out.

I suggest we intervene on our own behalf — and that we do it right now, in the present moment. When things begin accelerating wildly out of control, sometimes patience is the only answer. Press pause.

We have time for this.

-

Douglas Rushkoff, author, "Present Shock"

Douglas Rushkoff is the author of *Present Shock: When Everything Happens Now*, as well as a dozen other bestselling books on media, technology and culture, including *Program or Be Programmed*, *Media Virus*, *Life Inc* and the novel *Ecstasy Club*. He wrote the graphic novels *Testament and A.D.D.*, and made the television documentaries "Merchants of Cool," "The Persuaders" and "Digital Nation."

Learn more about Douglas Rushkoff at www.rushkoff.com

Chapter 2:

What Nobody's Talking About

by Cindy Gallop, founder, MakeLoveNotPorn

Sex. Death. Porn. Disease. We have a problem with communication.

The internet was supposed to make it easier for us all to engage in dialogues that were taboo before. We were supposed to be able to connect across borders to communicate in both private and public spaces, anonymous or fully tied to our own identities, about topics that perhaps we were uncomfortable discussing before. Perhaps we knew no one in person with whom we felt we could discuss them.

And yet we're no further forward than we were a long time ago. We're not getting more open. In fact, digital technology has really distorted things. And addressing this is fundamental to my own philosophies of both life and business.

I have a company called MakeLoveNotPorn (MLNP) which I started out of direct personal experience dating younger men: our tagline is 'Pro-sex. Pro-porn. Pro-knowing the difference.' I always have to explain to people that MLNP is not anti-porn. We are addressing the complete absence in our society of a counterpoint to porn – of an open, healthy dialogue around what constitutes "real world sex." Our mission is simply to provide a platform and tools that operate as 'sexual social currency,' to help people talk about sex -- talk about sex openly and honestly, both privately and intimately in their personal relationships, but also to engage with sex openly and honestly in the public domain. We want to make the discussion around #realworldsex socially acceptable, and therefore just as socially shareable as anything else we currently share on Facebook, Twitter, Tumblr, Instagram.

MakeLoveNotPorn the concept, the platform and the business is a manifestation of my own personal philosophies. I am all about communication -- my background is in the advertising industry. I've spent 28 years working in the business of communication, and that's why I believe that great sex is born out of great communication. Actually, communication is the key to everything good, in business and in life. The interesting thing is we often think we're communicating, and we're not, both publicly and privately. We have so many online tools available to us now, and we hear so much about oversharing and selfies and TMI and FOMO that we think our dialogue is more open than ever. It isn't.

This isn't just about sex, but I'll explain this with sex as a context. We all get vulnerable when we get naked. Sexual egos are fragile. People consequently find it bizarrely difficult to talk about sex with the people they're actually having it with, while they're actually having it. You're terrified that if you say anything at all about what's going on, if you make any comment on it, you'll hurt the other person's feelings; put them off you; derail the encounter; potentially even derail the entire relationship. At the same time you want to please your partner, you want to be 'good in bed', so if the only cues you've ever seen or been given are from porn, those are the cues you'll take – to not very good effect.

MakeLoveNotPorn.tv, launched a year ago, is my original 'Porn World vs Real World' site MakeLoveNotPorn.com brought to life: a usergenerated, crowdsourced videosharing platform that celebrates #realworldsex. One of our members summed our purpose up nicely when he said, "Watching porn makes me want to jerk off. Watching your videos makes me want to have sex." We're like any other social media platform – we're about connecting people, by opening up the dialogue around #realworldsex, to get to better sex, to get to better relationships, to get to better lives.

We have social agendas with MakeLoveNotPorn that address things nobody else is addressing. For example, because we don't talk about sex, we have no socially acceptable vocabulary with which to do so. The language of porn has rushed in to fill that gap – and that's not good, because as you would expect in a male-dominated industry, the language of porn is predominantly male-generated. The person who coined the term "finger-blasting" didn't have a vagina - because if you have a vagina and you hear the term "finger-blasting," you want to cross your legs. The person who coined the term 'Getting her ass railed', never got HIS ass railed. 'Pounding', 'Banging'….At MakeLoveNotPorn we're creating a new language for #realworldsex. We tag our videos differently, with terms like 'juicy', 'saucy', 'succulent'. Our term for 'oral' is 'downtown'. Our term for 'anal' is deliberately derived from the female experience – it's 'OwowowHEYNOW'. We want you to take our language and use it in the real world: publicly, so you never have to worry about being overheard or embarrassed at the words coming out of your mouth, and privately, so that you can say what you want in bed in a gender-equal, positive way, versus regurgitating the language of porn.

Something I've learned since starting MLNP is that there are other topics outside of sex that we also *think* we can discuss more openly thanks to social media -- but we can't. A few years ago I met a woman who was a fan of MLNP and who also happened to be a hospice worker. She said, "I deal with the same thing you do, because I'm in an industry that's also incredibly taboo to talk about: death."

She's totally right. We don't like to talk about death. We don't like to talk about our own mortality. We don't know how to talk about grief or condolences either -- Facebook doesn't have a "sympathy" button, just a "like" button -- and we have huge issues with discussion around serious or terminal illness. We just don't know how to deal with it. When a woman recently was lambasted by some high-profile news columnists for openly tweeting about her struggle with cancer, those columnists in turn were met with vitriol. A huge storm blew up around it. And that, to me, is indicative that this is a dialogue we don't yet know how to have, in spite of how much we think we can be open and honest through social media.

When we don't know how to talk about something, when we don't know how to articulate and communicate, we feel enormously uneasy and we find it very difficult to operate. Social media is all the same old human truths, instincts, attitudes, and dynamics -- just with a whole new methodology. All the same real-world dynamics play out on social media, just on a different platform. There's a distinct lack of ease with how you operate around these areas that you didn't feel comfortable discussing in the past, but now we're in a world where people are much more open through social media. And again, we haven't normalized that yet and people really struggle with how to speak, how to listen, and how to respond.

This, whether it deals with what we do in bed or not, is something we all have to address.

-

Cindy Gallop, Founder and CEO: MakeLoveNotPorn

Cindy Gallop is Founder and CEO of both MakeLoveNotPorn.com and ifwerantheworld.com. Entrepreneur, brandbuilder, marketer and advertiser, Cindy is constantly innovating.

Learn more about Cindy Gallop at www.cindygallop.com

Chapter 3:

Beyond the Human Being Operating System

by Aaron Balick, author, "The Psychodynamics of Social Networking"

Consider this: Your brain is an operating system. Let's call it the Human Being Operating System (HBOS).

Here's the conundrum we currently have: Today's culture has long surpassed the original programming that came pre-packaged in our HBOS. Although human beings are still pretty much on version 1.1, the operating systems of our digital technologies leap ahead, advancing at increasing speeds, clicking through system upgrades at a terrifying pace. How are we to keep up?

Lucky for us, our original programming is insanely complex and plastic enough to adapt to our accelerating technological culture — with some effort on our part. Still, our brains evolved within small hunting and gathering tribes, not the global network of information and communication that our technology presents us with by way of hardware and software.

We must not buy the line that our technology operates on a completely different register from our organic minds. In fact, HBOS underlies our technological advances at the most basic level – HBOS can be seen to be akin to the binary 0's and 1's that lay at the bottommost layer of all digital programming. After all, it was human beings who created technology in the first place, and we created it broadly in our image as an expression of our own needs and desires. Technology isn't something that has happened to us: our very human motivations were the spark that launched the technological revolution. Social shaping, the feedback loop that occurs between technological development and human response to it is essentially a relational project that keeps technology responsive to human needs.

HBOS, like all the operating systems in the living world, developed in response to the environment. One could say that the single most important question imbedded within the DNA of every living thing is, "How can I best ensure my survival (and the survival of my species) in this environment?" For humans and some higher primates, this involved the development of tools. For humans only, these tools developed into the highly sophisticated technology most of us have in our pockets today.

Our original programming came to realise early on that a networked environment was crucial for survival. In fact, the "social brain hypothesis" argues that there is a direct relationship between the size of the human brain and the cognitive requirement to manage complex social relationships. In other words, our brains grew so we could manage our social lives. Now we've developed tools to enhance this further; we've outsourced the social part of our brains.

With regard to our basic biological needs, we've had these tools covered for some time (think combine harvesters and mechanical dairy farming). The last decade and a half has now seen the follow-up technological enhancement of our complex relationships. In some ways this is a natural development of the Pony Express, the telegraph, and the telephone; but the new technologies that the Internet bring online far surpass these old connecting technologies.

The key take-home concept here is about *the extension of our psychological selves into the digital world by way of social networks*. In order to understand that, we need to look at the original extensions that already came kitted up with our HBOS.

The HBOS requires an extension of self in order to operate properly; the HBOS is inherently relational. When a newborn baby comes into the world, he is completely dependent on his mother or primary caretaker. (For purposes of simplicity I will use the pronoun "he" to distinguish the baby from his mother "she". Any individual who has a primary relationship to an infant can "mother" it, regardless of their gender.)

While it's obvious that this infant is dependent on its mother for his basic needs (food, water, shelter, and safety), what's less obvious is that he is also dependent on his mother's care. Put quite simply, babies do not thrive unless they are loved. The way a baby gets loved is through the developmental process of *recognition* by his mother. She *keeps the baby in mind*, comes to know his needs, and most importantly, feeds these needs back to him. This is the first extension of the self into another.

The way in which we seek recognition by extending ourselves into the minds of others continues throughout life. In other words, the need to relate to others is hardwired into the HBOS. And our technological plug-ins aim to continue and enhance this. At its very foundation, the internet allows us to extend ourselves into the desktops and smartphones of others, and hence their minds too.

We continue the process of psychological discovery through the relational means of social media, and in doing so, we express ourselves to larger audiences in a variety of ways.

However, social media interfaces are limited in the quality of information and the degree of aperture that is available for complex relating. Consider the amount of complexity offered between mother and baby; tone of voice, eye contact, touch, body language, body proximity and warmth; etc. In social networks, psychological recognition comes in the form of likes, comments, follows and re-tweets. Compared to interpersonal recognition, they are rather light on complexity: the aperture is narrow.

This narrow aperture gives many psychologists (and others) a fright. The fear is that we are limiting the ways in which people can relate to each other: that technology will ultimately undermine our relationships. However, it's important to keep in mind that in many ways the aperture is wider than it ever was. A communication across Facebook gives more information that a telegram ever could, and Skype has a wider aperture than the telephone. All the while human beings continue to relate to each other in real life all the time; our infatuation with our tools for relating sit atop an already complex system of human to human inter-relating.

Yet no technology is neutral. Technologies that offer a narrow aperture of interaction can invite an easier way of relating to others that can conspire to reduce the more difficult complex relationships that real-life offers us. When we cannot face the challenging relational feedback of vulnerability, conflict,or rejection, we may find ourselves leaning towards the narrower aperture relating-from-a-distance that technology offers us. If we lose the skills to deal with relational complexity, we might find ourselves in some serious trouble.

Nonetheless, "the future of now" is always in flux thanks to the neverending relational pattern of social shaping that will continue to alter the ways that social media technologies mediate our psychological lives. We might find that our technologies continue to change in a way that allows interaction through a wider aperture thanks to ways we have not yet conceived. As we extend further into the digital cloud, our manifestations of self will exist there in different ways.

One of the fundamental aims of the Human Being Operating System has always been to extend itself into the minds of others and to allow other minds to extend into our own -- keeping "the other" in mind is a core human trait. Thanks to technological tools, the HBOS itself has extended into a global network of interacting minds, and the social aspects of the Internet are simply a further extension of the social brain. Now, much of our social brain has been outsourced to the cloud. The development of this technology emerged from human will, and the psychological consequences of this are only just now beginning to be known.

-

Aaron Ballick, Author: "The Psychodynamics of Social Networking"

Aaron Balick registered integrative psychotherapist who offers psychotherapy, clinical supervision, and social networking consultation. He demonstrates his commitment to making these ideas more accessible through his book, "The Psychodynamics of Social Networking".

Learn more about Aaron Ballick at www.mindswork.co.uk

Chapter 4:

Stay Human

by Toby Daniels, co-founder and CEO, Crowdcentric & founder, Social Media Week

We get up in the morning and even before crawling out of bed, we check our phones for new notifications. As we grab our morning coffee, we turn again to social channels to fill the three-minute wait in line. More notifications. More likes. A few retweets and oh, an email and a text.

We judge those people. Out to dinner, we see that couple, heads down focused on their phones, forgetting to interact with one another. Then, in a moment of brilliant wit, we turn to Twitter to post about the sorry sight (while inadvertently mimicking their posture). Your friends follow suit, favoriting and retweeting -- but let's revisit the word "friends"? When was the last time we actually interacted with them, anyway?

We admit it. We've done it all.

Our phones buzz constantly. The red notification has permeated our lives – on our laptops, on our phones – it begs for attention; begs us to drop everything to find out what lies on the other side of the lock screen. Along the way, technology became our closest friend, the one we would do anything for, drop anything for, even break away from a genuine human conversation to be with.

There is a reason this friendship first developed- in many ways, our new relationship with technology is positive. We are now able to connect with friends around the globe, making distance a forgettable obstacle. The average American moves every five years, so tech allows us to keep up, no matter where we might go. Tech can empower us. There are tools that can help us optimize our day that allow us to create cognitive maps, establish a disciplined routine for social media engagement, and develop more meaning within our relationships. We're seeing this already emerge in the fields of quantified self and wearable tech and we expect that we will see more of it.

But we should not forget about technology's dark side. We see families who can't put down their phones at dinner. We make light of "the breakup text", but we all know someone who has been on the receiving end. Work is only an email away, making vacations and time off a distant memory. Phones buzz; emails alert; but we're never satisfied with what we get or where we are. FOMO (fear of missing out) cripples our ability to live in the moment and across the board, we're seeing an increase in stress-related disorders. We are conditioned for overstimulation and overscheduling, causing the kind of chronic stress that leads to behavioral, mood and attention disorders.

We have shortchanged our future for immediate gratification.

Yet, when we delay gratification, we increase our overall success, social competence, and happiness in general. Our 24/7 connection to the digital world often disconnects us from the real world around us — our physical surroundings, our loved ones, and especially ourselves. We become over-stimulated, left with fewer resources to devote to what really matters to us: our goals and our relationships.

But we don't have to let technology treat us this way. We can still have control. When we understand that nothing is more important than how we engage in the present, we can start to focus more on the positive, productive and human-centric side of this wonderfully complex thing we've grown to love so much.

As we consider the ever-increasing role that technology plays in our lives, it's worth asking: What really separates us from technology? It's compassion; recognizing the difference and sameness of others. It's seeking out connection with others. It's understanding our own emotions and behavior and experiencing the depth of our daily lives — both challenges and joys. Famed psychologist Carl Rogers defined humanness as living in the moment, fully open to the experiences we encounter in our lives. As a "fully functioning person," you will be able to express feelings freely, trust in yourself, and live a rich, full, creative life. We possess an outward need to relate to others and express ourselves, but we also have a need for inner meaning and purpose. You may recall Maslow's hierarchy of needs — up at the top of his pyramid of needs, lays purpose and meaning in life. Technology is a tool, beneficial only as it helps us lead lives of meaning.

I sum up being human as living with intention and expression. And with that, I'll leave you with a quote from one of life's great philosophers, Ferris Bueller.

"Life moves pretty fast. If you don't stop and look around once in awhile, you might miss it."

-

Toby Daniels, Co-founder and CEO: Crowdcentric

Toby is the co-founder and CEO Crowdcentric, designing a future where technology and humanity come together to create a more open, connected and sustainable world. Crowdcentric Media owns and operates Social Media Week, a leading media platform and worldwide event that captures, curates and shares the most meaningful ideas around technology and social media's impact on business, society and culture.

Learn more about Toby Daniels at www.crowdcentric.net

Chapter 5:

Games in the Gheralta

by Brooke Hammerling, founder, Brew PR

There are a lot of things you can learn -- about yourself, about the world, about humanity -- from traveling to a place like Ethiopia. I just hadn't expected one of my most profound lessons to involve a game on an iPhone.

I was in Ethiopia for the first time ever, going as part of my work with charity:water, and we were staying in the Tigrai region to the north of the country, near the Gheralta mountain formation. It's the kind of breathtaking, mountainous place that reminds you that the birth of civilization was literally right here. There are ancient rock paintings, churches carved right into the cliffs, and broad valleys where people still live in the mud huts that they've been building for millennia -- and where the sunrises and sunsets are some of the most spectacular in the world.

One morning I decided to climb up on one of the ridges and snap some pictures of the sunrise and the valley with my iPhone. I was sitting by myself, looking out ahead, no one around me, and focused my camera -- and that's when I realized I wasn't alone. Out of the blue, a little girl from the village below appeared right next to me from behind a rock, looking at me with curiosity and inquisitiveness. Or, rather, she was looking at the odd, glowing little device in my hand. I wasn't surprised, seeing as there was a very good chance she'd never seen anything like an iPhone before. So I held my phone out to her so that she could see it and touch it. I opened up a basic game app and used it to show her what a touch screen was like.

And here's what blew me away: Within about five minutes, she was playing the game on her own. She understood the rules. She and I sat there for half an hour, playing this game together, laughing together even though we spoke almost none of each others' languages. It was a conversation, one we wouldn't have been able to have over a deck of playing cards or a book. This technology that connected us wasn't something cultural, it was something human. And I was deeply moved. The funny thing is, some people I know would've told me that for that whole trip I should've had my smartphone stashed in the bottom of my bag to use for mobile boarding passes on my flight home and nothing else. But having it with me brought me an incredible experience.

Flash forward a few days and I was back in New York, back to my life working with tech startups large and small at Brew PR, back to a world where being constantly connected to technology meant hectic moments like frantically trying to finish typing and sending a text on my iPhone before the rush-hour subway I'm riding barrels into a tunnel with no cell reception. It was a far cry from that magical experience on a mountain ridge in rural Ethiopia. And in one particularly hectic moment, maybe in between midnight emails with clients, I wondered how the heck I could get that experience back -- or at the very least, how I could learn something from it.

At Brew PR, my team and I work with lots of tech company founders, some of whom are seasoned executives and some of whom are leading businesses for the first time in their lives. And the young ones, especially, are absolutely tethered to technology. They're working harder and more intensely than, I think, any prior generation of professionals -- and it's not that prior generations didn't work hard. But their work lives were dictated by the 9 to 5 schedule. There wasn't a buzzing BlackBerry going home with them. Life outside the office literally was work-free in most cases. With entrepreneurs, they're doing so much work during the day that when they finally leave the office, it's time to pay attention to all the emails they didn't have time to send during the day. We use our cell phones as alarm clocks, and the moment we wake up in the morning we're grabbing them and checking Facebook. I have friends and clients who can't stop from checking their emails or Instagram accounts at dinner parties. I've seen people become so addicted to the "always-on" life that they don't even realize how disengaged they've become from their surroundings.

I'm pretty guilty of some of this myself. So it serves as a personal reminder to me, too, when I pass along the Brew mantra of "work hard, play hard" to our entrepreneurial clients. Play hard, whether that means you're going to go climb a mountain, or lie out in the sun on the beach, or spend a chunk of out-of-office time working with charity:water in Ethiopia. And I don't think there's any shame in wanting to Instagram that experience, in wanting to share it with friends back home while you're there. It's not about being connected or being disconnected. It's about using our connected lives for meaningful things -- whether it's productivity on the job or bringing us closer to family and friends both old and new.

What I brought back from Ethiopia is that understanding and managing the technology closest to us is about that balance. There are so many times when our personal tech is isolating us, not connecting us. And as I learned sitting on a rock in the Gheralta Mountains, those connections can be moments that cross cultures, generations, and even languages.

-

Brooke Hammerling, Founder: Brew Media Relations

Brooke Hammerling founded Brew Media Relations to provide media relations, strategy & networking to amazingly cool tech companies.

Learn more about Brooke Hammerling at www.about.me/brookehammerling

Chapter 6:

Neighbors

by Leah Busque, founder, TaskRabbit

About a year into founding TaskRabbit, a company designed to easily hire people to do small jobs or errands for you, we received an email from a user that completely changed our perspective on what we were building. And it also changed my personal perspective on how technology is really redefining who your neighbors are and who you can rely on.

We'd just launched our second TaskRabbit city -- San Francisco, where I'd just relocated from Boston, our first city. The email was from a Bay Area-based mother whose 20-year-old son was going through chemotherapy treatment at Massachusetts General Hospital in Boston. She's a librarian and didn't have the funds to fly across the country to be with her son during this traumatic time, so she turned to TaskRabbit to see how she could build a support system.

She ended up posting on TaskRabbit that she needed someone in Boston to go visit her son every day in the hospital for a week, to bring him healthy meals and cozy blankets, and to sit with him for 30 minutes a day and call her afterward to give her the update on how things were going. The TaskRabbit who picked up the job, it turns out, was also a mother, and the bond between these two people formed across the country became a powerful one. We tell this story internally a lot so that everyone at TaskRabbit knows the things that can happen when people find new ways to connect with neighbors, old and new. It keeps us motivated and focused on what's possible.

If you look back, when the internet and the World Wide Web were first gaining mainstream adoption, people were finding new and exciting ways to connect. Maybe you lived in a small town and didn't know anyone in real life who shared some of your interests; now you had communities that you could turn to. But sometimes this went further than we would have wanted it to. We became siloed, anonymous screen names and avatars were common, and online communication gave us a reason to not connect face-to-face.

Facebook, the first mainstream service to really push the idea of tying your online identity to your real identity, turned 10 years old in 2014. And in these past few years technology has really started to catch up and mimic real-world human behavior. Something that's innate in all of us is the desire to connect and to relate as humans, to help each other out and to be part of something. Finally, technology and internet platforms are at a place where we can leverage them to help bring communities back together; it's not just TaskRabbit, but a lot of companies from Airbnb to Lyft. We're giving new generations that have been brought up on the internet a new way of building neighborhoods and building communities, and redefining what that means in this day and age.

Believe it or not, this was all a surprise to me. When I founded TaskRabbit, I was living in Boston, which is obviously a great college town, and I was expecting that most of the people who would want to be TaskRabbits would be college students with some extra time on their hands who wanted to make a bit of spare cash. But that wasn't the case -- as it turns out, our now nearly 20,000 TaskRabbits in the U.S. come from all age groups and educational backgrounds. (75% of them have a bachelor's degree already, which means that a lot of them are past their college-kid years.)

Why did things turn out this way? Sure, when TaskRabbit launched it was late 2008 and economic concerns certainly drove many people to seek freelance or supplemental employment, but I think a deeper reason is that people found this strong, perhaps unconscious desire to be part of their real-life communities again. Online, we've become accustomed to being able to be part of figurative "neighborhoods" based on our interests and affinities. There's real value in meeting like-minded people, whether it's something quirky (like fellow Doctor Who enthusiasts) or more serious (someone dealing with the same chronic disease) and the internet's been enabling that from the early days of IRC chat. But there's also incredible value in meeting the diverse people who are right around us.

We have one TaskRabbit who's a brain surgeon. No, he doesn't perform brain surgeries on people who hire him as a TaskRabbit -- he's a skilled handyman and also loves picking up research jobs as well. He probably is pretty busy with his day job, but he's eager to pitch in and meet some of the people around him in the process. That's what I find so motivating about new technology as a whole, not just TaskRabbit: Helping people become members of their communities in a way that we have forgotten over time.

-

Leah Busque, Founder and CEO: TaskRabbit

Laura Busque is a Boston Native Engineer turned San Francisco entrepreneur. She is Founder and CEO of TaskRabbit, a community of people joining together to get things done.

Learn more about Leah Busque at www.taskrabbit.com

PART 2
The Fight for Our Attention

Chapter 7:

Surviving the Bankruptcy of Our Attention

Craig Hepburn, Global Director of Social and Digital, Nokia

The web is currently going through the biggest change since search revolutionized how we navigate and find information, products and services. At the same time, we are experiencing an unprecedented transformation in how we consume and share digital content. More content will be created and shared in the next year than in all of history and that's both exciting and challenging. In the past decade we've seen the rise of smartphones, apps, sensors that understand the world around us, and data that promises to soon transform how we buy, experience and more importantly discover new products and services.

And if you're a Talking Heads fan: " You may ask yourself -- well -- how did I get here?" and if you're just generally curious, you may also ask yourself "So what?" and "Why should I care?". Especially if you're in the advertising business.

If you're an entrepreneur, investor or a company in middle of all this disruption and change, the reason is simple: As the amount of content being produced and shared increases so does the number of ways consumers can filter out the noise that is irrelevant and not personally relatable. We are entering the "attention economy," and this is where the next wave of major innovation will be focused.

Herbert A. Simon was perhaps the first person to articulate the concept of attention economics when he wrote:

"...in an information-rich world, the wealth of information means a dearth of something else: a scarcity of whatever it is that information consumes. What information consumes is rather obvious: it consumes the attention of its recipients. Hence a wealth of information creates a poverty of attention and a need to allocate that attention efficiently among the overabundance of information sources that might consume it."

As content and information becomes increasingly abundant and immediately available, attention becomes the determining factor with regard to whether information is consumed or not, and entrepreneurs and businesses that understand this will be the ones that win.

A number of software applications either explicitly or implicitly take attention economy into consideration in their user interface design, based on the realization that if it takes the user too long to locate something, they will go elsewhere. Some writers have even speculated that "attention transactions" will replace financial transactions as the focus of our economic system of the future.

The internet helped solve many of the financial challenges over the past 20 years by providing solutions and infrastructure to be more efficient as a human race. Search then solved the issue of time and finding information. But we are now facing the challenge of human attention, which will be solved in part by the rise of social discovery and recommendations by trusted sources and influential networks.

This brings me to why I believe that companies and brands over the next few years will need to solve two key challenges: One, building influential advocate communities that both share and create content on behalf of brands; and two, the mechanics of content discovery that grab the attention of consumers.

Let's visit that first point. There's been a lot of talk about influencers and brand advocates for a long time now, and one of the issues is that we haven't quite figured out the metrics for it yet -- or even whether there is a standard metric. Who's a better advocate: Someone with 50,000 Twitter followers who may as well just be anyone, or someone with 2,000 Twitter followers who are truly paying attention to what this supposed "influencer" says? To what extent can the idea of influence or advocacy change over time on behalf of one individual? Our brand advocacy can change with our location, with our age, even with the seasons.

Discovery also remains a problem. Until recently, customized versions of content -- let's take news as an example -- primarily involved checking some boxes to tell a website what you liked to read about. Don't really care about sports? Then don't check the "sports" box. But sometimes even someone who doesn't give a hoot about sports will have reason to connect with content around it, and that's where there are still advances to be made in allowing our technologies to reflect the fluidity of the human brain's thought processes and our fast-moving society. The concept of discovery, like the concept of a brand advocate, is ultimately more nuanced that we initially believed, and as our always-on, always connected world continues to mature into something commonplace rather than a novelty, this will become ever more evident.

At the end of the day, human relationships and trust have not evolved, but the technology of advertising content has moved forward at such an incredible pace that we have moved beyond the realms of human content consumption. Our brains no longer even process information with which we don't currently have a relationship directly or through our own human networks.

This is why the rise of social advertising, where content from existing human relationships and networks will converge with branded commercial content and services, will transform the advertising business.

-

Craig Hepburn, Global Director of Digital & Social Media, Nokia

Craig is Global Director of Digital & Social Media at Nokia, responsible for leading a world class digital and social media team. Craig was voted as one of the UK's rising stars in the digital marketing sector by Revolution Magazine, shortlisted for digital person of the year by the DADI awards and contributes to many publications on social media and digital marketing.

Learn more about Craig Hepburn at twitter.com/craighepburn

Chapter 8:

The Daily You

by Michael Nutley, media consultant

In the past 20 years media in the developed world has moved from scarcity to glut, and news is one of the best examples of the change. In the old, pre-media fragmentation, pre-internet days, news on TV was strictly rationed to three doses a day; lunchtime, early evening and late evening. And there were newspapers and magazines, almost all paid for. And that was about it.

Now news is everywhere, and it's almost all free. And the focus of attention, for digital-savvy consumers at least, is how to cope with the surfeit. How do you find the stuff you're interested in among all the noise? And who do you trust to get rid of all the stuff you don't want to read?

Because the other thing that has happened is that news has been atomised. Just as music is now consumed by the track, news is consumed by the story. Bundling, whether in the form of albums or newspapers, is out of fashion.

Back in 1995 Nicholas Negroponte, digital thinker and co-founder of the MIT Media Lab, predicted the internet would usher in "The Daily Me," a precisely tailored news vehicle with an audience of one. Nearly 20 years later, that prediction is coming true, in two forms. There's socially-curated news, of which Twitter is the best example, and there's machine-curated news, such as Flipboard.

Both of these approaches atomize the traditional news bundles and deliver to you only the items that interest you. Both approaches require some work - choosing the right people to follow or the right outlets and categories to pull items from - but what's interesting is that for at least a section of the population, putting that work in seems preferable to actually paying somebody (for example, a newspaper editor) to do it for you. In this news outlets seem to be experiencing the same shift that advertisers have seen. People's trust in advertising continues to plummet, at least in mature markets, while the views of "people like me," expressed in social media, are extremely persuasive.

The other great benefit of social curation is that it solves the problem of serendipity. The search-based, algorithm-driven aspects of the internet increasingly drive you to things in which you've already expressed an interest. Because social curation involves human beings in all their diversity, you never know when someone you're following is going to recommend something you never knew you'd care about.

But there's a problem with both of these approaches to curation, and it's that they amount to a kind of secondary editing. A secondary or citizen editor can take stories that have been created elsewhere and give them prominence to his or her own readers or followers. Very little of the material promoted by citizen editors or their automated counterparts is actually created by them.

The rows about whether this remarketing of news benefits its creators or damages them have been going on for several years and show little hope of stopping any time soon. The secondary editors argue that they are bringing the stories to a wider audience, therefore generating traffic. The publishers say that secondary editing actually reduces the importance of their sites, as these sites are no longer the primary source of news. Social media in this case acts as proof of Oscar Wilde's axiom that the only thing worse than being talked about is not being talked about. What's certain is that it's not going to stop anytime soon.

In the meantime, news outlets continue to struggle. Revenues from digital outlets aren't replacing those lost in the decline of analog products, and the industry continues to shrink as wave follows wave of cost-cutting. And it's a downward spiral. Falling revenues force cost cuts, which impact on quality, which in turn further discourage readership and depress revenues, whether from advertising or direct payment.

In an attempt to fill the gap, publishers find themselves diversifying their offerings in ways that stretch from the obvious (conferences, shows) to the more exotic (the proliferation of dating services in UK broadsheet papers in recent years isn't due to the publishers' concern for their readers' love lives). They're also attempting to find advertising formats that drive better revenues than traditional banners. Hence the rise of "native advertising" - what used to be known as advertorial - and other experiments on the boundary where editorial and commercial interests meet. A few publishers are also implementing "paywall" digital subscription strategies, which seem to be working rather well in a few cases and likely quite poorly in others.

The fact remains that the curation functions - both human and machine - broadly rely on other people to write the stories they curate and aggregate. And if the companies that pay those writers go out of business, there'll be a lot less content to curate (full disclosure: I've been a journalist for 29 years, so this isn't entirely an abstract argument for me).

It's worth remembering that there are many different kinds of news, produced under different circumstances. And this diversity is throwing up different business models in different areas, all of which will increase in importance.

The most obvious new approach is to get people to write news for you for free -- or rather for increased social standing and peer respect rather than actual money. This is part of the basis of the Huffington Post, and it's also being trialled by U.K. local paper group Johnston Press, whose Bourne Experiment aims to source three-quarters of the editorial from the community in one of its local papers. And a similar approach is being developed at U.K.-based publisher UBM, which is using websites to keep the conversations among visitors to its trade shows going beyond the few dates that shows are open. But in the U.S., this strategy has been going on for some time and has proven not just controversial but also not necessarily successful, as a few "citizen news" experiments have flopped spectacularly and lost venture capitalists quite a bit of money in the process.

We're also seeing a lot more brands declaring themselves to be media properties, implicitly or explicitly. Often it's hard to get them to explain what this actually means, but for others, particularly B2B brands, are developing and funding media properties, and paying journalists to write for them.

There's also the possibility of taking on the curators at their own game, by being so niche and so expert that you're the de facto choice for news about that niche. As my former deputy editor used to put it: "Are we indispensable to our readers?"

These approaches look likely to proliferate in specialist and B2B news, where communities turn to experts and where brands can position themselves as facilitating the discussions. But how much national or international news you can source this way looks questionable. What looks likely in the short to medium term is more experimentation, more innovation and more hybrid approaches as publishers look for ways of creating content on lower budgets.

And the issue remains: While the benefit of curation is what's not there, someone still has to pay for the content that is.

-

Michael Nutley, Media Consultant

Michael Nutley is an independent consultant and writer specialising in the business use of interactive media. He is the former editor-in-chief of New Media Age, the UK's leading source of news about interactive marketing and media.

Learn more about Michael Nutley at www.twitter.com/mikenutley

Chapter 9:

If Cats Could Play Miley Cyrus

Jonah Peretti, founder, BuzzFeed; in conversation with Elisa Kreisinger, fellow, Eyebeam Center for Art & Technology

Eyebeam Fellows are artists, hackers, and engineers who spearhead new research and develop exciting new work at the point where art and technology meet. Jonah Peretti formerly directed R&D at Eyebeam and he is interview by current Eyebeam fellow, Elisa Kreisinger.

ELISA KREISINGER: Unbeknownst to me, I've actually been following your work since I was a teenager, and I had no idea any of it was you. There's a simplicity to your work that really inspires me. You're like a mad scientist of complex things like social sharing and spreadability but you somehow boil it down to make it simple.

JONAH PERETTI: There is some aspect of the scientific method to it. Not in a rigorous sense, but it's about what you were saying before about the simplicity of the work. Part of the reason for that simplicity is that you're trying to eliminate variables to try and actually learn something. When you are doing work that has so many different pieces to it, it's hard to know what's happening. But when you can eliminate as many variables as possible and get down to something that's as simple as possible, that's when you learn.

EK: It's really hard to do that. As an artist here at Eyebeam, I struggle to do that. But that's what good art is.

JP: For me, my motivation started even earlier than my time at Eyebeam, with the Nike emails and "Black People Love Us." And it wasn't to make works of art. The main motivation was to entertain people, or provoke people or make people think about an issue. And I was also trying to understand human behavior, and how media spreads and how ideas propagate and spread. And that's not the mission of most artists. They aren't trying to do an experiment, they are trying to make their art work. So that simplicity helped with that mission in particular, which is a little different from that of most artists.

EK: Like you said, you wanted to provoke people to think about an issue. That's the role of art. It's not necessarily to be popular and spread. There's a perception that if art spreads and it's popular, it's not good.

JP: I think that fine art, or art in the gallery system, has a complicated relationship with popularity. If something is too popular it almost makes it not art, unless it becomes a meta-commentary on popularity, you know, like Koons or Warhol. I talk a lot about this with Cory Arcangel, because back in those Eyebeam days we did a few projects together and you know, he's incapable of making a viral hit on the web in part because everything he makes ends up feeling like art. Even when we collaborated together and made things that were kind of interesting, they were always less clear than the kind of work I do on my own, but it seemed more like art. They were better as art than they were as pop culture.

EK: Were they popular? Just out of curiosity? Did people like them and share them?

JP: I would say they were popular if you looked at it through an art lens. In terms of how many people saw it? Thousands of people liked it and it was well-reviewed in shows and galleries. But they weren't popular from a contagious media standpoint. He made this video of Schoenberg's Cat, which were clips from YouTube of cats stepping on a piano and then he played a challenging contemporary classical music-like piece with these clips. I was like, "Cory, that's so brilliant, but if you had done it with 'Party in the USA' by Miley Cyrus, it would have been this huge thing that got million and millions of views!' And he's like 'Well, I can't really do that.' It's like, the cats and YouTube and lowbrow culture with a great work of challenging music that made it into something that felt like art and it was probably 'pop' from a gallery standpoint, but from the perspective of the kind of stuff I do, it couldn't achieve escape velocity and get shared across the Internet. It was too complicated and too heady and too hard for the average person to understand.

EK: I agree. I love work that's highbrow meets lowbrow. You're steering people who have traditionally turned towards pop culture kind of away from it, and those who have turned away from popular culture a little more towards it. So it's this positioning to get both sides of the aisle to kind of look at the same thing from two different perspectives. Ideally.

JP: Yeah, you're causing people to reflect on things they might not reflect on, and you're challenging people.

EK: I'm sitting in the studio space at Eyebeam now. What was your time here at Eyebeam like?

JP: That was an amazing time in my life when I was at Eyebeam. We had all this space, and we didn't have much budget, but there was a tremendous amount of freedom. It was in a period after the dotcom crash, but before there was any kind of hyper-excitement about startups, and so there were all these people who were interested in the Web, in technology and in open source, art, graffiti and DIY hacking. We were all working on various projects and kind of collaborating on things where there was mutual interest. It didn't look like art that you'd be trying to show in galleries and it didn't look like a company or a Web startup or a product. It just felt like people messing around but now if you do these kinds of things, people try to hire you or fund your startup.

EK: Not really! Well, maybe they do, but I'm here in that position and I still mostly just get asked if whether what I do is legal, or told that I must just have a ton of free time on my hands.

JP: Yes, I think maybe that the stuff you're doing now, in 5 or 10 years, will become a bigger part of what the media industry is. Consider things like ReBlog, which we developed at Eyebeam as an open source project that let people click on a little "re-blog" button that indicate to share content they liked into their own stream. That concept became part of Tumblr, and became part of Twitter as the re-tweet. At the time it was, open source software you had to install on your own server and set up and link blogs and others through RSS and it was super clunky and difficult, but it turned out to be an important gesture of how people share content. It was an early precursor to things that people are doing now. It's hard to predict the future, though. So who knows what people will be doing in 10 years.

EK: Yeah, totally. It seems like your time at MIT MediaLab and Eyebeam, that time to experiment and create and just have drop-in type of community where you could play around and mix stuff and not have an outcome and not have a goal in mind, just kind of make what was needed, was key to your career trajectory -- not even your career, just what you love and what you want to make.

JP: It's kind of a paradox, because it's not like any of us there were doing this for our career trajectory. We didn't know where any of this stuff was going to lead, and I think having spaces where people can play and experiment helps people work out ideas. I think one of the challenges you see in the startup world is that people drop out of school and start a company, or they start it soon after they graduate, and when their startups take off (if they're among the lucky ones who take off), they don't have anything to draw on from previous experience of playing with ideas and experimenting with different approaches. And not only do I want to draw upon that experimental approach, I want to bring it into BuzzFeed too.

EK: I never thought of that -- BuzzFeed is now sort of a container for experimenting, just like Eyebeam was for you. A way for you to keep working with cool ideas, but in a different context.

JP: I think because of the Eyebeam experience, when I'm thinking about things at BuzzFeed, I often take into account things I learned years ago during that period of all that experimentation. There are all kinds of ideas that come back from when they were nascent and a period of where we are not actually trying to build anything or have a particular outcome, but just trying to learn and explore. I sometimes will come up with an idea, like recently we posted the full text of a Wittgenstein book on BuzzFeed, and it's gotten over 100,000 views. It's this dense philosophical text and yet, it's gotten all these shares on Facebook and Twitter. It was this kind of experiment -- has BuzzFeed grown enough that we can post an extremely challenging philosophical text and see it get traction?

EK: Someone once asked you why things are shared and why do certain pieces of media spread, and you said there are a few criteria. That it needs to somehow be provocative or shocking -- and it has to be broadly appealing enough that you want to send it to your whole address book. I've always considered my feminist and queer video work to be niche, but in a post "Girls"-era maybe it's not so niche. Maybe those communities are now considered broadly appealing.

JP: Part of what I was wondering was, how do you make something that seems controversial and shocking but still be something you could send to your contacts in your address book? If something were truly controversial and shocking, it'd be hard to send to everyone you know because you'd offend them. It's this weird thing -- we want novelty and things that feel a little shocking and controversial, but only if they can really be shared. Now, that's a tricky tightrope to walk. Like, if "Black People Love Us" had been so controversial and racist that when you shared it, people would write back to you in horror, then it wouldn't have spread. But if it was totally uncontroversial and didn't make a statement in any way, then people wouldn't have any reason to share it. So when I said that I think I was in a moment when I was trying to think through this oppositional thing of people want things that are shocking and controversial *and* the things they can share, but most of the time people share things that aren't controversial because otherwise you get in trouble for sharing it.

JP: But to your point about LGBT and feminism and writing things that are about a group that aren't necessarily in mainstream consciousness. The good news is that a lot has changed and in particular when you look at LGBT content -- it's some of the most shared content. The work that we did on the Sochi Olympics controversy in Russia, and the marriage equality content we've done over the past few years, is very widely shared. And apart from that particular area, we've seen that content that ties into people's identity is shared at a really high rate like, "Signs You Were Raised By Asian Immigrant Parents," or "The Challenges of Being Left Handed." Facebook's architecture for sharing is an identity-based one, where you know you can share stuff on Facebook and it'll reach people you're close to, who may likely be interested in that content too. So if you really care about gay rights or a particular political issue or if you are left-handed or were raised by Asian immigrant parents- that is going to give you added motivation to share. Whereas if it's just something broadly interesting, you're not going to share it on Facebook. I think content tied to identity is actually becoming a new class of extremely popular content.

EK: So people will share content that appeals to their specific identities rather than something that is more of a broad pop culture reference.

JP: What's interesting is that the Asian immigrants parents post was shared a lot by people who grew up with Asian parents, but the majority of people who saw it weren't Asian. We could look at Quantcast data and see that only 40% of the people who saw it were Asian -- part of the reason why they were sharing is to explain to their non-Asian friends what their childhood was like. You see people's identities being an anchor for sharing, but they're sharing with other people that can learn from their experiences.

EK: So it becomes a tool for commonality-based sharing -- you post it on your timeline and have an instant conversation starter about growing up with Asian immigrant parents with people with whom you normally wouldn't have this conversation with.

JP: For example, during Thanksgiving, BuzzFeed's UK office passed out maps of the outline of 50 states of the US and asked people to fill them in. There were all these hilarious maps created by Brits who had no idea where different states were located on the map. Our UK team posted that and it was huge, both in the US and overseas. We quickly did one in the New York office where we had New Yorkers try to fill in maps of Europe. All of Eastern Europe were labeled with stuff like, "I don't know! I'm so, so sorry!" So it was about specific things that mattered to people, and about identity. But it was also about reaching out in a humorous good-natured way and connecting to people who are different.. Identity matters but you also want a mutual understanding. Instead of having authoritative pieces of content that unite everyone, you are seeing more empathetic media where people are trying to understand and empathize with each other.

EK: I agree.

JP: So you empathize with that!

Jonah Peretti, Founder and CEO: Buzzfeed

Jonah Peretti is Founder and CEO of BuzzFeed, a media company that provides a pioneering mix of breaking news, entertainment and shareable content. After co-founding The Huffington Post in 2005, Peretti launched BuzzFeed in 2006 as an experimental lab that focused on tracking viral content and making things people wanted to share.

Learn more about Jonah Peretti at www.buzzfeed.com

**Elisa Kreisinger, Artist and Fellow,
Eyebeam Center for Art & Technology**

Elisa Kreisinger is a Brooklyn-based video artist whose work includes remixing pop culture. Her latest videos mash up Mad Men into feminists and The Real Housewives into lesbians.

Learn more about Elisa at www.popculturepirate.com

Chapter 10:

Trapped by TL;DR

by Seth Godin, author

This was republished with permission from Seth Godin's blog, where it was originally posted on January 8, 2014.

TL;DR is internet talk for "too long; didn't read." It's also a sad, dangerous symptom of the malfunctions caused by the internet tsunami. (For a most ironic example of this paradox, read the lengthy, droning edit discussion on the Wikipedia article for, yes, "too long; didn't read.")

The triathlete doesn't look for the coldest bottle of water as she jogs by ... she wants it fast and now. That mindset, of focusing merely on what's fast, is now a common reaction to many online options. I think it works great for runners, not so well for learners.

There's a checklist, punchline mentality that's dangerous and easy to adopt. Enough with the build up, wrap this up, let me check it off, categorize it and quickly get to the next thing ... c'mon, c'mon, too late, TL;DR ...

Let's agree on two things:

1. There are thousands of times as many things available to read as there were a decade ago. It's possible that in fact there are millions as many.

2. Now that everyone *can* write, publish, email you stuff and generally make noise, everyone might and many people already are.

As a result, there's too much noise, too much poorly written, overly written, defensively written and generally useless stuff cluttering your life.

When we had trusted curators it was easy. We read what we were supposed to read, we read what we trusted, regardless of how long it was, because the curator was taking a risk and promising us it was worth it. No longer. Now, it's up to us.

One option is to read incisively, curate, edit, choose your sources carefully. Limit the inbound to what's important, not what's shiny or urgent or silly.

The other option is to assume that you already know what you need to know, and refuse to read *anything* deeply. Hide behind clever acronyms, flit from viral topic to flame war, never actually diving in. It appears that this is far more common than ever before.

Here's what I've found: When I read in checklist mode, I learn almost nothing. It's easy to cherry pick the amusing or the merely short, but it's a quick thrill with very little to show for it.

Judging by length is foolish. TL;DR shows self-contempt, because you're ignoring the useful in exchange for the short or the amusing. The media has responded to our demand by giving us a rising tide of ever shorter, ever more amusing wastes of time.

Short lowers the bar, but it also makes it hard to deliver much.

Please, give me something long (but make it worth my time).

Perhaps a new acronym: NW;DR (not worthwhile; didn't read) makes more sense. We've got plenty to choose from, but what we need is content that's worth the effort.

-

Seth Godin, Author

Seth Godin is the author of 17 bestselling books around the world that have been translated into more than 35 languages. He writes about the post-industrial revolution, the way ideas spread, marketing, quitting, leadership, and, most of all, changing everything. You might be familiar with his books *Linchpin*, *Tribes*, *The Dip*, and *Purple Cow*.

Learn more about Seth Godin at www.sethgodin.com

PART 3
Innovating With the User in Mind

Chapter 11:

Getting Past the Long, Dark Scandinavian Winter

by Nathan Eagle, founder, Jana

Slightly over a decade ago, it wasn't uncommon to see students walking around MIT's campus who had literally strapped desktop computers to themselves as backpacks or were wearing giant head-mounted displays. This was the Wearable Computing Group, and it didn't help that they referred to themselves as "the Borg." They were collecting really interesting data about themselves, but also serving as a means of amusement for the rest of the student body watching these guys waddle around with computers attached to their backs.

In the early 2000s, the idea of wearable computing — of enhancing our personal experiences and, in turn, what we can learn about ourselves through technology — was pretty weird even by MIT's standards. I showed up in 2001 as a bright-eyed, over-eager masters student, and when I joined the Borg, I was pretty keen to figure out some way to avoid the inevitable social stigma of spending my graduate career dressing up like a computer. But on a less superficial level, the fact of the matter is, the members of the Borg were basically only able to monitor, and program, for themselves. Those massive apparatuses would never be relevant to the overwhelming majority of people in the world. And I wanted to understand the many, not the few.

Luckily for me, that was right around the time that Nokia launched its first mainstream programmable phone, which used a language called Symbian. I made a deal with my adviser, Alex "Sandy" Pentland, to be allowed to program this phone to capture similar types of data to my Borg colleagues. Sandy thought it might be a worthwhile avenue to pursue, and I became one of the first few mobile phone programmers. This wasn't glamorous. I could get access to the Bluetooth chipsets, the cell radio and, in some instances, I was able to start logging key presses. That's about it.

But even with that really coarse data you can generate some extraordinary insights into individual behavior. Nokia began sponsoring my research, donated 100 handsets to the project, and I started hacking on a little app that would run in the background to log these things. This was well before GPS was in handsets, so we couldn't do anything with GPS, but we could see the

ID of the cell tower that the phone was affiliated with, so we could get coarse estimates of location and, subsequently, movement. We could start predicting where people might have dinner and even with whom they might have dinner — with the most rudimentary of programmable cell phones over a decade ago. It was clear to me that this would ultimately get much, much bigger.

How things have changed. As technology grew and evolved, I joined the faculty at MIT and started getting into much, much bigger sets of mobile phone data, and into population-level behavior. Then, I started working with mobile phone operators to help them analyze their datasets of tens, if not hundreds, of millions of people. The operators that needed the help the most were not in this country or in western Europe, but in emerging markets who were inundated with petabytes of data from subscribers whose numbers were exploding. They knew there was intrinsic value there; they knew they needed to understand the underlying dynamics of the subscriber base, but it was just too much data. And that's how I was introduced to the complicated, incredible world of mobile devices in emerging markets.

In countries like the U.S., Finland, or Korea, I didn't think mobile phones were necessarily having the impact on peoples' lives that I envisioned they could have. I envisioned them changing peoples' lives for the better and fundamentally empowering them in a wide spectrum of ways. But I was seeing that in Africa. In emerging markets, the average mobile phone subscriber spends 10 percent of his or her entire income on prepaid airtime — and airtime is literally a currency in these markets. Mobile phones are telephone connections, radios, flashlights, and ATMs. Suddenly, these handsets are bank accounts for people who have never visited a bank. The impact this $50 piece of plastic can have on the life of a rural Kenyan woman is more than most people in the developed world can even imagine.

Although mobile phones were having a massive impact on the lives of Africans, if you were to look at the handset and the applications on it, they were more than likely designed by some developer in Finland suffering through a long, dark Scandinavian winter. It seemed pretty weird given that the end user was a farmer on the equator trying to figure out market prices or weather patterns. There was a real disconnect between the people designing the products and the people who were using them. The developer in Finland, the thing they're focused on, is how to get a phone Bluetooth-synced with Microsoft Outlook to try to get calendar apps to update faster. These are very much first-world apps and features that a business executive in North America really values. And they're what the developed market prioritizes.

The answer eventually became obvious: African mobile devices are best when programmed by Africans themselves. Nokia ended up sponsoring my creation of a mobile phone programming curriculum to be deployed across sub-Saharan Africa. We had more than half a dozen computer science departments incorporating it in countries from Senegal to South Africa. The idea was pretty simple. Teaching African computer scientists to develop apps for themselves, for their families, for their communities — mobile apps by Africans for Africa — really took off.

It's amazing to see how much interest there was from the students about learning how to program these handsets. You get all sorts of extraordinary, real innovation. Emerging markets prioritize radically different features that the developed markets would never think of. One of my students, for example, built an airtime regulator — basically like a SCUBA regulator, but for a mobile phone. His mother lived in a rural village outside Nairobi that required about a two-day walk to buy scratch cards for more airtime. He built something for her phone that would cut the phone off after she spent something like 10 shillings' worth of talk time so that the next day she would have another 10 shillings and wouldn't have to go make that walk to buy more airtime. She'd buy bulk airtime but then get it in increments every day, which helped her manage her finances as well as prevent her from ever become stranded without the ability to communicate.

Wearable computing devices, whether Google Glass, the latest generation of iPhone, or some massive contraption worn on the back of a member of MIT's Borg, achieve their promises when they're programmed by somebody who understands the end user. Mobile technology has already transformed emerging markets from India to Ethiopia, and it's going to continue to do so — but the priorities are wildly different in the markets there. When local developers are empowered to build their own mobile apps, the end results are incredible, going significantly above and beyond what we could even imagine these markets want or need.

The fact that a developer in Finland connects to the same internet as a cattle rancher in Kenya can be deceptive. They're connected in the same way, for the most part, but when you look at population-level data to dig deeper into understanding the core needs of why mobile devices are so important to us, the differences are even bigger than we may have thought. That long, dark Scandinavian winter might be the ideal environment for fueling the creativity to build new address book syncing apps (for when people feel productive) or avian catapult-launching games (for when they don't). But the best environment for creating the apps that are going to continue to spur momentous change in sub-Saharan Africa is sub-Saharan Africa itself.

-

Nathan Eagle, founder, Jana

Dr. Nathan Eagle is the cofounder and CEO of Jana, the world's largest rewards platform. With integrations into the billing systems of 237 mobile operators, Jana can instantly reward 3.48 billion emerging market consumers in 70 local currencies.

Learn more about Nathan Eagle at www.jana.com

Chapter 12:

Trust Through Anonymity:
A Look At The Chinese Internet

by Tricia Wang, ethnographer and sociologist

People aren't surprised to hear that social media habits in China are different from the way that they are in the U.S. or the U.K. But what surprises them is why. "Because the internet's censored?" most of them ask.

The answer, actually, is no. It's more complicated than that, and it's rooted in something much older.

There's so much about the China, where I've done quite a sizable portion of my work as a tech ethnographer, that baffles the world.

The first thing that Westerners need to understand about social media in China is that the concepts of friendship and trust are completely different there. China is known as being a very low-trust society. The Communist regime made reporting on friends a duty to the party. Every individual was tracked by a dossier that documented many things, including what people reported. People started reporting on friends, and even family members. This destroyed personal trust because it made every suspicious of each other. And sharing information became a very dangerous and risky act. The safest thing to do in this social context was to remain silent.

After the Chinese economic reforms of 1979, the concept of friendship really changed--a friend became someone who could get you something through a back door. Essentially, friendship was a transactional economic relationship. It's not how Westerns define friendship as a non-instrumental and authentic relationship.

The second thing that Westerners need to understand about social media in China is that censorship doesn't affect Chinese internet users as much as you think. That's the big finding of my research after a decade of living in and out of China. And this really counters what we hear in the West, and what journalists and even most academic research tells us -- that Chinese censorship hinders people's ability to find information and gets in the way of their ability to carry on with their lives.

I always get asked, "What is it like for a whole country that can't access Facebook or Twitter?" For one thing, they have their own platforms that they're using, and their platforms are really fulfilling because they offer relevant features that can't even be found on Western platforms. The constraints of censorship force people, too, to come up with new ways of getting around things. For example, Sina Weibo, which is like China's version of Twitter, is heavily censored, which means that people do have to be a bit careful about what they post. But one of the things that came out of this constraint is a third-party app called Long Weibo that turns text into a .JPG image to embed into a Sina Weibo post, preventing algorithm from detecting any of the words in it because it's an image. This innovation is a practical response to the constraint of 140 characters because Long Weibo allows people can post things that were simply too long for Sina Weibo's Twitter-like character length -- like recipes, for example. It's created a means of creative expression that has nothing to do with getting around censorship regulations.

One of the most transformative effects of social media in China is that its created a space where people are able to talk to each other and interact anonymously. But it's key that whether we're talking about China or any other region of the world, we can't talk about "social media" as something homogeneous or monolithic. If we do, then we miss the fact that some social media platforms are better for formal interactions and other platforms are really good for informal interactions. Formal interactions are found on platforms like Facebook where you have to use your real name with your known contacts; other platforms like Tumblr are more informal, where anonymity and experimentation are encouraged. Many other sites fall in between. In China, social media sites that are dominant in informal interactions, like Weibo (where you don't have to use your real name) or QQ (where you have the option of using a pseudonym), or forum sites that are basically equivalent to Reddit or 4chan, we're seeing trust being established between strangers and relationships emerging that look a lot like friendship.

The lesson to be learned here about any culture, not just China, is that the way we interact online is deeply rooted in societal norms that go back decades or even centuries. And none of this has anything to do with turning on a mobile device or opening an app, but it does influence how these devices and apps are used. The way we engage with social technologies anywhere is closely rooted in what constitutes a friend or a contact and how we trust people around us (and people far away). Our desire to gravitate towards informal social media platforms is connected to how we've historically viewed social spaces from coffee shops to town squares and cosmopolitan cities-- we've always been open to meeting strangers.

Once we understand that, we can see how new kinds of relationships are unfolding in places all across the planet -- and learn from both our similarities and differences. As always, if you're trying to engage a new community or serve a new market, you'll do yourself a big favor by seeking to understand it first.

-

Tricia Wang, Global Tech Ethnographer

Tricia Wang is a tech ethnographer transforming how organizations understand people and conduct research. A Fulbright Fellow and National Science Foundation Fellow, Tricia has been recognized as a leading authority for her work specializing in integrating balanced data practices to fulfill business & institutional goals that improve people's lives.

Learn more about Tricia Wang at www.triciawang.com

Chapter 13:

If It Will Work In Africa, It Will Work Anywhere

by Mark Kaigwa, Kenyan mobile and media consultant

"You probably don't have much use for more than one SIM card in a single mobile device where you're from." Bobby cheerfully says. A blogger based in Nairobi, he keeps two phones himself. Besides his Android dual-core smartphone, he keeps what he describes as a "mulika mwizi" phone. The phrase is a humorous expression that loosely translates from Swahili to mean "shine a light on a thief." The metaphor's origin, coming from a popular Kenyan song of the same name, refers to the flashlight capability of his basic Nokia phone. With his battery life going close to a month with every charge, and the phone offering a built-in radio in addition to that flashlight, it's not hard to see why it's important to him. "I wouldn't be caught dead without it."

In America, two mobile phones -- let alone dual-, triple-, and even quadruple-SIM card devices -- might be an annoyance, but in Africa, it's a solution. When it comes to technology and mobility, Africans have proved ingenious at finding workarounds to make up for where their technology is lacking, and their solutions are starting to become globally visible. With a population of just over 1 billion people, there are over 700 million mobile phone subscribers in Africa's 55 countries. This is only expected to grow.

Africa tells the story of a continent embracing mobility and rapid change. By 2030, there will be more Africans living in cities than there are in all Western countries' cities today. According to World Bank statistics, 11 of the 20 fastest growing economies globally are in Sub-Saharan Africa. "Africa Rising" has been the subject of conferences, conversations and communication around the world.

Beyond the headlines of rapid economic development, infrastructure, and natural resources lies a more interesting narrative: Mobility as a pioneer for innovation. Africa has seen ideas come not from hubs of resources, ideas and development but from the fringes and the edges. It's often posed that more Africans have access to mobile phones than to electricity itself -- in 2009 it was estimated that there are more mobile phones than lightbulbs in Uganda. That's a far cry from the 1990s, when a widely circulated (albeit disputed) statement claimed that there were more phone lines in Manhattan than in the 55 African countries combined. The mobile revolution changed that.

Many an African today will experience the internet for the first time on a mobile phone. But they're often not the LCD, multi-color touchscreen devices that the West is used to. The tech developments that make waves in Africa often involve SMS -- yes, text messaging. The very definition of email is changing as Gmail and Google search have been offered over SMS to keep up with this, unlocking new potential for what can be done on a two-inch monochrome screen. But, obviously, there are constraints. And it is these same constraints that prove a breeding ground for innovative ideas to take shape.

Wikipedia, for example, has chosen not to restrict access to its tomes of information to those with internet access -- regardless of whether it is a feature-phone with basic, text-heavy internet access across its small screen or a "dumb-phone" with no access at all. A pilot by the Wikimedia Foundation is exploring Wikipedia Zero which makes access free and creates an SMS-powered version of the popular web encyclopedia, potentially opening access up to well over two billion people across the world who otherwise have not had it. As you can imagine, this is a big deal in Africa.

Other Africa-focused innovation has been centered on leapfrogging the infrastructural problems where the continent has traditionally lagged the Western world by far. Patchy cell phone coverage and fluctuation of electricity, for example, isn't uncommon in African cities (even in cities, cuts to the fiber-optic cables from large urban construction projects or ships at coastal ports can cripple connectivity), and frustration over this is what birthed the BRCK, developed by Ushahidi and described as a backup generator for the internet. Built for the city and the village alike, the rugged device can switch between WiFi, 3G/4G, and ethernet to provide nonstop connectivity thanks to an 8-hour battery.

The challenges BRCK takes on and the pain points it addresses might not hold as much water in London or New York (unless you're off out of town fishing, that is) but in Bangalore, Bamako, or Brasilia they make a great difference. Mobile connectivity continues to have some teething problems as cities connect and citizens join the grid; basic infrastructure has yet to fully match the speeds of growth that mobile has brought with it. To some this is frustration, to others it leads to frugal innovation that leads to ideas like BRCK.

Or there's Google's Project Loon, which takes to the challenge of connectivity on the continent from a different perspective -- the challenge of offering internet to areas where the network or infrastructure has not developed. Project Loon, currently being tested in New Zealand, puts solar-powered balloons at the stratospheric level to provide 3G signal to the most remote of areas. Given that the challenge for Africa has continued to be the last mile of connectivity, with devices becoming increasingly affordable but access in landlocked countries still keeping prices high, the sheer scale of an idea like Project Loon could usher in a new age of connectivity across the continent.

Projects like Loon were obviously conceived outside of Africa. But technology manufactured on the African continent holds the same nimble, mobile philosophy. In 2013, African tablet manufacturers began bringing African-made, Africa-focused technology to the table -- like the Way C, the first African-designed Android tablet, a dual-SIM device built by a Congo-based entrepreneur. Africa's ushering in an age designing less with a "mobile-first" mindset and more with a "mobile-only" one. Even though upward mobility means that devices, design and development should anticipate upgrades to a richer and more interactive experience, the philosophy supersedes the medium.

Most Westerners get their African tech news from the occasional Economist lead story or Fast Company feature. But this barely scratches the surface of interpreting how frugal innovation and design thinking are beginning to frame, analyse and solve the challenges of the "next billion." An ongoing relationship with African digital influencers like Bobby, getting slices of day-to-day life in this new age of global mobility, can offer a deeper perspective.

The phrase "getting some Africa in your timeline" couldn't be more appropriate. In an age where everyone's seeking the next great idea, lessons in ingenuity, inspiration and mobility may come from where you'd least expect it: Africa.

Mark Kaigwa, Kenyan Mobile and Media Consultant

Mark Kaigwa has spent the last 7 years helping global and African businesses, brands and nonprofits use technology to connect with Africans online. As a consultant, strategist and speaker, Mark likes to get hands-on solving problems and applying ideas that will change the continent of Africa's future and the future of emerging markets.

Learn more about Mark Kaigwa at www.mark.co.ke

Chapter 14:

When Handwriting Recognition Saves Lives

by Catriona Campbell, founder, Seren

Doctors tend to have terrible handwriting. In fact, many assert that they have the worst handwriting of any profession in the world.

This is, actually, more than just common knowledge. Actual academic studies, like one 2003 paper in the American Journal of Managing Care, have come to the same conclusion: doctors' handwriting is abnormally illegible, often stemming from situations where patients, caregivers, or pharmacists have a difficult time reading it. And this poses an interesting and surprisingly significant problem as the medical industry works to join the 21st century with all its promises.

Another thing about doctors is that they normally share data, findings and knowledge at symposiums, sometimes only once a year. And in journals. This is obviously not ideal. One doctor may discover that a new treatment works unexpectedly for a patient, potentially even saving a life in the process, and wouldn't be able to share that knowledge with others in the field for a full year. Yet doctors are constantly keeping handwritten notes about symptoms, medicines prescribed and patients' progress, normally kept in a patient's hospital room so that any doctor or nurse on duty can check them. Think about the possibilities if this kind of data (anonymized, of course) were digitized. A doctor could instantly check to see if a patient's reaction to a treatment was expected or unexpected. He or she also could tap into bigger datasets amassed from medical professionals around the world that could offer massive amounts of previously unforeseen knowledge.

This was the thinking when Microsoft commissioned Seren, the user experience agency I founded, to help them understand how digital could aid patients and their recovery process in hospitals across the UK and Europe. We had ambitions to test handwriting recognition software in tablet PCs to digitize the content of those notes that doctors took and to create a docking station at patients' bedsides to send the data to a central hospital database. The idea was that if each hospital ran a similar system, data could be amassed across hospitals and across diseases to unlock new discoveries and perhaps even new cures.

Among our observations was just how much patients' mental well-being is improved when they had the ability to share their illness and recovery process online. Digital media in hospitals proves to be just as game-changing for patients as it is for doctors. The online forums, many of them run by medical charities, where patients from far-flung places can share information about their illness — or where parents can learn and share information about a child's illness — are becoming increasingly useful for self-diagnosis and the spread of knowledge. This, for me, was an example of social media truly proving a benefit to the world.

But when it came to attempting to make medical professionals adapt more easily to a world of digital and sharing, things did not work out for a surprising reason: Doctors' handwriting was simply too much for the handwriting recognition software to handle. Technology's supposed to aid us and improve our life and work, not force us to undergo time-consuming new processes like attempting to alter one's handwriting so a machine can read it better. The handwriting recognition technology had not, and still has not, caught up to with the ability of the hardware — and the doctors we worked with just weren't convinced of the efficacy of the software because it was taking so long to learn how to read their handwriting.

Out of all the things we talk about when it comes to developing technologies, handwriting recognition and other user experience issues aren't the sexiest of them. They aren't drone-copters or 3D printers or wearable anything. But it's crucial to understand user experience, because day in and day out, we see amazing technologies that just aren't as suitable as they ought to be for the audience at hand — the usability of the system around the handwriting recognition in our research case wasn't appropriate for the users, who were doctors. Or think about air traffic control systems. They haven't been updated in terms of the applications and the software they use for about 20 years, so our lives are in the hands of controllers who are reading off screens that may as well be from the MS-DOS age. The user experience is absolutely appalling, particularly when you realize that the quality of user experience in flight simulator video games is leaps and bounds ahead.

There is a positive side to all this. Amazing things are being created. The Microsoft Game Center in Seattle is doing phenomenal work with regard to the design standards around gaming, and these developments can (and should) make their way to other fields where they can very much impact improvements in user experience. Think about the Halo franchise, which wasn't just a blockbuster hit — it could be played in more or less every country or culture regardless of background, even soaring past language barriers thanks to tests and trials with users from all over the world.

But these findings can't just be restricted to entertainment. One of the amazing things about all the fast developments in technology we're experiencing is that a development made by one field might be crucial to another. Perhaps the secret to better handwriting recognition user experience is found somewhere in Xbox or PC game software, and perhaps then that hopeful vision for a shared database of medical knowledge can be realized.

Catriona Campbell, Founding Director, Seren

Catriona Campbell is Founding Director of Seren, a customer experience consulting firm. Catriona was one of the first inductees to the UK Digital Hall of Fame for services to digital design, accessibility and User Experience.

Learn more about Catriona Campbell at www.seren.com

Chapter 15:

Culturability

by Nathalie Nahai, author, "Webs of Influence"

We hear a lot about personalization on the web -- from predicting personal preferences and human behaviors, to assessing psychological persuasion techniques, with methods ranging from anthropology to big-data crunching. The internet is becoming an increasingly personalized place, but there's one fundamental area that has remained, to date, dangerously overlooked -- and that's culture.

This nebulous, intangible thing that we call "culture" is profound and inescapable in how it influences the people we become as we grow up. In a 2002 article in the Journal of Information and Computer Systems, S. S. Robbins and A. C. Stylianou defined it as *"a shared set of values that influence societal perceptions, attitudes, preferences, and responses."* Our culture shapes our entire experience of reality -- the way in which we perceive and interact with the world, with our peers, and with ourselves, both on- and offline. And often, this is subconscious.

And when it comes to online experience, culture shapes the way in which we search for, understand and interact with websites and other media. Given that the Internet is a Western invention, based on the Roman alphabet and Western ideals of aesthetics and usability, it was initially predicted that we would move towards a homogenized web – one in which we'd all speak the same language (English) and express the same, standardized set of preferences for design and development.

This reality didn't materialize.

But how could a single website work so well in one culture, and fail so miserably in another? Well, as it turns out, different cultural groups employ different usage strategies when using the same interface4. This means that if I were to present the same website, in your mother tongue, to you and to a fellow reader in, say, Latvia, you would both (subconsciously) interact with that site in very different ways.

In 1998, W. Barber and A. Badre defined a concept called "culturability" -- "the relationship between culture and usability in WWW design." As we transition further into a world of constant global connectedness, this is a key and often seemingly contradictory concept that will only grow in importance.

The best place to start in understanding culturability is to look at a country's macropersonality traits. Geert Hofstede, a Dutch professor of social psychology who spent over 40 years exploring the subject, defined culture in his 2010 work *Cultures and Organizations: Software of the mind* as "the collective mental programming of the human mind which distinguishes one group of people from another".

From his years of extensive research, he distilled 6 key cultural dimensions that we can use to describe, measure and compare different countries -- power distance, masculinity vs. femininity, uncertainty avoidance, pragmatism vs. normative, and indulgence vs. restraint. (It's worth doing an internet search for "Hofstede's dimensions" to learn a bit more.)

How do these play out online? Well, let's take four countries as examples: the UK, Finland, Japan and the USA.

First, the UK and the USA. Perhaps unsurprisingly, according to Hofstede's dimensions both of these countries have very similar scores across the board. They score pretty low for power distance -- which Hofstede defines as "the degree to which the less powerful members of a society accept and expect that power is distributed unequally" -- and both cultures express highly individualistic and masculine traits ("a preference in society for achievement, heroism, assertiveness and material rewards for success"). Brits are slightly more uncertainty-embracing than their American peers (hence both cultures are quite innovative), and the scores show that each nation is generally short-term-oriented and indulgent in their gratification of natural drives.

Online, this often translates into a preference for websites that offer equal access, have a looser structure, and are easier to explore. Since both cultures place a high value on earned media (such as likes, ratings, reviews, testimonials, etc.), making businesses more social to leverage this fact can have a dramatic impact on their perceived credibility and conversions. They can also use the UK and USA's short-term orientation to make their marketing or advertising campaigns more effective with competitions that offer excitement and immediate gratification.

With the exception of a low power-distance score and a short-term orientation, Finland scores quite differently from the USA and UK across the other traits. It is less individualistic as a nation, and its culture is very feminine – placing a greater value on quality of life (liking what you do) than on keeping up with the Joneses (being the best). In general, Finns are moderately uncertainty avoidant, meaning that they tend to express a preference for rules and stricter social norms.

This translates online as an increased desire for security, more explicit, structured navigation, and website images and content that reflect socially acceptable scenes and behaviours. A great example of this is the clear, structured interface of the website huuto.net, a social marketplace site in which users can buy and sell products within the community (a bit like eBay). As a culture, the Finns are only slightly less indulgent than the UK and USA, which means that online you can entice Finnish users with messages that convey fun, enjoyment of life, and the gratification of natural urges (such as feasting, dancing, sex…)! This is so commonplace that 'love and sex' even has its own section in the primary navigation of one of their top news websites: iltalehti.fi.

Finally, let's take look at Japan. Famous for (among other things) their rich cultural heritage of Zen gardens, minimalist design aesthetics and tea ceremonies, when it comes to websites, the Japanese couldn't be more different. In terms of traits, as a culture they rank as mildly hierarchical for power distance, and they tread a balance between collectivist and individualist. While the harmony of the group is considered more important than expressing individual opinion, the fact that Japan has one of the highest masculinity scores in the world means that you often find extreme competitiveness between groups. It's also one of the most uncertainty-avoidant cultures, which means that life tends to be highly ritualized and risk factors are always taken into account before any decisions can be made.

Online, these traits can be leveraged by making websites interactive, exciting and dynamic, within a structured, predictable framework -- and loading them with detail to help uncertainty-avoidant Japanese web users get informed and come to decisions. Since the Japanese language is so complex and information-rich, its speakers are used to processing huge amounts of information very rapidly. Which is why if you're designing or visiting a Japanese website, you'll find that they appear (to Western eyes) to be incredibly chaotic, cluttered and visually overwhelming. While it may be too much for other cultures to take in, the visual cacophony of Japanese websites are in fact finely tuned to reflect the preferences and needs of their audience – you can see this evidenced in the bright, loud interface of rakuten.co.jp, Japan's largest online shopping mall.

Now, all of this may well be a lot to think about, and indeed culture is anything but simple. But if we are to optimize our online endeavours so that we can succeed not only now, but in the future, then *culturability* may just turn out to be your most powerful tool yet. If you are building things on the internet, you are now developing for a global internet. Smartphone access in emerging markets is continuing to drive new users online at an incredible rate, so it's now more important than ever that we understand how the cultural context of our users are influencing their online preferences and behaviors. To put it another way, if you want to convert and communicate effectively online, you need to know how to leverage culturability.

Nathalie Nahai, Author: "Webs of Influence: The Psychology of Online Persuasion"

Nathalie Nahai, The Web Psychologist, is author of best-seller, "Webs of Influence". In her work, she studies how online environments influence our attitudes and behaviours.

Learn more about Nathalie Nahai at www.thewebpsychologist.com

Chapter 16:

Antuyo

by Michael Kleiman, filmmaker, "WEB"

"Don't forget about us, Michael," Mauricio pleaded. His eyes locked with mine, braving the glare of the harsh Andean sun that served as my key light. "The rest of the world always forgets us. But you…you remember."

I had been living in the small village of Antuyo, nestled deep within Peru's Andes Mountains, for approximately two months. I was there to make a documentary film, *Web*, about the introduction of laptops and Internet access to remote villages via the One Laptop Per Child program. In addition to documenting the effects that technology had on such communities, I wanted to capture the process of connection as we've known it for thousands of years – two strangers coming together face-to-face, sharing meals, exchanging looks, laughs, and stories, and growing to care for each other. As we try to digitize that process, I wondered, how does our very understanding of connection begin to change? Do we lose something of ourselves in the transformation?

I lived with two families: Mauricio's family, who lived way at the top of the mountain (*Arrrrrriba!* -- as they liked to say) and Bernardo and Roy's family, who lived at the bottom of the hill. Bernardo and Roy, 12 and 5 respectively, served as my enthusiastic tour guides in Antuyo, teaching me how to build and fly kites in the open valley below their home, treating me to freshly harvested sugar cane, showing me the proper way to herd a donkey up the mountain, and stepping in as my speedy saviors when -- sensing my weakness -- my donkey ran away and sprinted toward freedom. Each family was kind enough to offer me a bed, blankets to shield me from the cold mountain air, and as much of the local cuisine as I could ever care to eat. At home, over dinners of potatoes, spaghetti, and occasionally guinea pig (a delicacy in the Andes), the adults of Antuyo would indulge the many curiosities they had about my life in New York.

"Is life here the same as life in your country?"
"How much does a cow cost in your country?"
"If I wanted to come live in the United States, could I?"
"What would a plate of guinea pig cost in New York City?"

I answered their questions as best as I could ("I've never tried to sell a cow, to be honest." "Coming to the U.S. can be very difficult and very expensive." "We don't eat guinea pigs, we keep them as pets – a sort of animal guest in our home.").

I quickly felt at home in Antuyo. I spent two or three days each week filming in the one-room primary school, as students explored their new laptops. The kids discovered various games and taught one another how to maneuver and solve the endless puzzles the machine provided.

It was not long before they stumbled upon Wikipedia. They were blown away by the access to information and their ability to leap from link to link, each a gateway of discovery. An initial search for information on Planet Earth lead the children to the pages for the solar system, stars, the sun, trees, the Amazon. A few days later Bernardo, who loved music, stumbled upon the Wikipedia entry for music. His face lit up with wonder as he traversed entries about different types of music stemming from all over the world. The subsequent journey through these myriad digital wormholes led him to the "Mona Lisa."

"Do you know what this is?" I asked him.

"God," was his response. I told him to read the article. "Oh, it's Mona," he said as if recognizing an old friend. I smiled as his eyes remained glued to the page. My own mind dwelled on the many treasures left for Bernardo to discover and the new ones he'll undoubtedly share with us all.

In addition to the moments I documented on film in Antuyo, there were many others that could not be captured by my camera. Like in the first hours of the morning, when the mountains blocked the sun's dominance of the sky, creating the illusion of a battle between the peaceful night sky and the sun as it pushed the moon and stars away with all of the power of its daylight. There were small triumphs of joy when I climbed trees with Bernardo, who sang the whole time, and remembered again what it was to be a kid with nothing to do but get dirty, play and be home before dark.

There were, of course, moments of difficulty and foreignness, times when I felt of a different world. But above all, what I learned from my time in Antuyo is that while we all inherit different lives -- different challenges posed to us that are met with different reactions -- we are above all else the same. And while this appearance of other often clouds our vision and ability to see the undeniable truth of similarity that is at our core, when we demand that our eyes see through this fog, the world offers to us the greatest of its gifts: connection, a bridge between two worlds that allows us to learn, to understand, and to grow.

"Don't forget about us, Michael."

I found Mauricio's eyes with my stare and wondered how I might respond to a request so small and yet so large. Should I explain that in my world we cannot forget? Should I describe the flood of connections and memories and friend requests and push notifications that, though birthed in my world, is rapidly inundating his? Should I lament for all we stand to lose in such a wave, or triumphantly proselytize the progress that will come when our worlds are forever bound?

"I'll never forget you," I promised in a whisper, my mind overwhelmed by the image of Bernardo and Roy charging through an endless field, kites flying high above them, their shrieks filled with the joys of childhood.

-

Michael Kleinman, Filmmaker: WEB

Michael Kleinman is the Co-founder of Righteous Pictures whose most recent film, WEB, premieres February 2014. Michael was also producer and co-director of RP's award-winning debut "The Last Survivor".

Learn more about Michael Kleinman's work at www.righteouspictures.com

PART 4
Changing the World Through Technology

Chapter 17:

Transforming Sport, Transforming Society

by Richard Ayers, founder, Seven League

"Sport has the power to change the world…it has the power to inspire. It has the power to unite people in a way that little else does. It speaks to youth in a language they understand. Sport can create hope where once there was only despair. It is more powerful than government in breaking down racial barriers."

That's Nelson Mandela, inspiring as he ever was.

I don't have the ability to inspire like that – nor do I claim to have the sporting skills to be able to play or coach at a serious level. I am a journalist turned geek – I just happen to love everything about the sporting world. Two years ago, when I started our company Seven League, it was because I could see not only that sport transforms society but also that digital can transform sport.

We have, of course, already seen this transformation start. "Always on" and "always connected" means that we're living in what marketers call an attention economy, and brands of all stripes have scrambled to get in front of consumers on a dozen or more newly relevant platforms. That means that some very large and established organizations often have to go far outside of their comfort zones; in the dot-com era people referred to 'passion centers' such as music, film and sport as the hubs of human attention -- and sport is way up there.

Just look at Twitter's 'most tweets per second' milestones, and you'll see that the majority of them came from sporting events; or note that sports stars like Cristiano Ronaldo and Lebron James top the charts for facebook fans; or that a 19-year-old bloke from North London called KSI can have 4.2 million subscribers to his YouTube channel because he happens to be a big gamer and Arsenal football fan. Clever people at Google and Microsoft and Apple spend a lot of money and mind power figuring out how to engage sports audiences. They're that powerful.

But as our world grows more constantly connected and digitized, tweets-per-second will prove to be the most basic of metrics and Facebook fan pages a decidedly low-tech sort of hub. Some of the issues getting tossed around the Seven League office right now are connected stadiums and the use of 'complementary' or second screens. What will we be able to do when we can start to assume and accept ubiquitous connectivity? That's where things are really starting to transform.

And then, once you have the connectivity, there's the hardware. The big buzzphrases here are "internet of things" or "ubicomp" (ubiquitous computing). Think about products like Google Glass or the much-more-sporty Recon Jet. These waves of technological development will have a big impact on how we integrate sport into our lives – and how our lives feedback into sport. Not because you can read your email in a heads-up display while mountain biking, but because of the data transference – part of the growing quantified self – that means our understanding of ourselves, computers' understanding of us, and by extension other peoples' understanding of us, will grow and grow.

It works both ways as both an (amateur) athlete and a fan: I can monitor my performance, but I can also monitor a sports star's performance and then compare the two. Suddenly there is a whole new level of appreciation that can be engendered, and from that, new levels of inspiration.

Sports stats have traditionally been the preserve of the uber-nerd, and more as a tool for tribal exclusion rather than inclusion. In the US, where Nate Silver rocketed his way to celebrity through his mastery of baseball statistics, sports coverage uses data much more than most European sports (especially soccer), but the tide is changing here too. We feel passionately that sports stats can be used in far more entertaining ways to reach new audiences, whatever their level of knowledge. Using the data to make it entertaining as well as compelling -- we call this "Dataitainment" – can be a powerful force in encouraging people to play, attend, and follow sports, especially niche sports or those where video rights aren't available.

When we were children we imagined being part of moments of greatness. Jumpers-for-goalposts or re-enacting a great catch. The ability to experience a champion athlete's own moments of greatness is getting closer with initiatives like RefCam in Major League Soccer and rugby – but combine that with "datatainment" and the quantified self, and you can go so far as to know the player's heart rate…or even *feel* his heart rate. You could know what it's like to be on the pitch – using Xbox's Kinect or augmented reality, or some other new kind of display that we haven't even dreamed up yet. Wouldn't that be thrilling? Wouldn't that drive fans on to seek that same natural high of excitement and experience?

With digital media's ability to connect with individuals very personally – whether that's because it's in your pocket, or because it's using your friends' recommendations – no longer does a media outlet have to pick one audience to focus on. Now, they can have one conversation with those who may be new to following a sport with little knowledge of it, and at the same have a different conversation with the expert fan. With this comes the improvement in device cameras and the aforementioned ubiquitous connectivity where anyone can share what he or she is seeing – and that leads to greater participation off the field as well as on. The audience of the near future will form an army of reporters, photographers, camera operators, and editors who may never see or speak to one another but who are all equal parts of a sensational whole. The potential for mass collaboration means the next Olympics or World Cup will have to find ways to facilitate this sharing and to harness this power to communicate for the benefit of the sport.

Mr Mandela spoke of sport's power to transform. Our feeling is that the combination of new technologies, real-time communications and social media with the powerful, socially-transforming cultural institutions of sport means that new frontiers await us.

Richard Ayers, Founder and CEO: Seven League

Founder and CEO of Seven League, Richard Ayers is a hybrid of content and commercial expertise. 7 League is a is a digital media firm, specializing in sport with clients like Manchester City FC and Major League Soccer.

Learn more about Richard Ayers at sevenleague.co.uk

Chapter 18:

How to Save Marketing

by Rory Sutherland, Vice-Chairman of Ogilvy and Mather UK

This essay was adapted from Rory Sutherland's essay in Wired UK magazine in June 2013.

If the digital age has done nothing else for productivity, it has proved spectacularly effective at generating a supply of mantras.

For those of us old enough to remember the incunabula of the web, it is occasionally worth pausing to remember a few mantras often heard in the mid-90s, and to ask how well they have survived the test of time. Like this one, which always stuck with me because it was made with such confidence: "There will be no customer loyalty on the internet, since a cheaper price is always just one click away."

That was almost universally believed at the time. In the late 90s it was rare to read an article in a business publication that did not predict that online shopping would degenerate into an orgy of price-comparison sites linked to a plethora of online retailers. What do we see in reality? In fact a kind of inverse-square law seems to operate: the largest online retailer, Amazon, sells nearly five times more than its nearest US competitor, Staples.com, and ten times more than Walmart.com. In the UK its dominance is even more pronounced (I am excluding the online grocery services here, since the supplying of perishable goods is unavoidably different).

Why were all the economists so wrong on this question? Or, to paraphrase Her Majesty the Queen on the financial crisis, "Why did nobody see this coming?" Well, it's only fair to say there are some perfectly conventional economic reasons why Amazon enjoys this supremacy. Its prices by and large are highly competitive.

It offers enormous choice. Its service is good. And it benefits from scale in its warehousing and in its negotiations with suppliers (though certainly no more than Walmart, which owns Asda). It also profits from other network effects, for instance, in the volume of customer reviews it attracts and in its appeal to marketplace sellers. But are these the only reasons? None of these post-rationalisations can on their own adequately explain Amazon's dominance. If, as economists believe, people really do check competitive prices before buying a book from Amazon, it doesn't explain why no one much even bothers to compete in the categories Amazon dominates. Try searching book titles on Google if you doubt this.

What if the biggest reasons for Amazon's supremacy are not economic but psychological -- the product of the cognitive short-cuts we adopt while facing an influx of data presented to us in everyday situations?

There is a mental bias whereby we are inclined to adopt a course of action simply because it easily comes to mind. Note that this is not the same as simple "awareness" or "fame." After all, Staples and Walmart both enjoy equivalent name recognition to Amazon in the US. "A brand's mental availability refers to the probability that a buyer will notice, recognise and/or think of a brand in buying situations," says Byron Sharp, professor of marketing science at the University of South Australia. "It depends on the quality and quantity of memory structures related to the brand."

He continues, "This is much more than awareness, whether that is top-of-mind awareness, recognition or recall. Indeed, all of these [conventional marketing] measures are flawed by the use of a single, a-situational cue."

So, regardless of overall fame or reputation, context matters. When I'm offline, whether I go to Tesco or Waitrose may depend on the time of day, my location, mood and a host of other variables, all of which cause me to distribute my retail spending across a plethora of brands. When online, these variables are far fewer; hence the winner-takes-all effect (sometimes called the "Matthew Effect", named after the passage in that gospel where it is suggested that those who already have, inevitably get more) is not diminished by the ease of comparison and switching. On the contrary, it's more extreme.

It is difficult for any physical retailer, even Asda, to enjoy physical proximity to all its customers. But mental proximity is a different matter. You can effectively monopolise that.

Yes, sometimes we do what economists believe, and assiduously check every possible retail outlet to find the lowest cost. But, let's face it, our lives would be intolerable if we evaluated every alternative before doing anything. We rarely test-drive more than two cars before we commit to buy one, so why should we search hundreds of web pages before buying a DVD? Instead we fall back on a simple, default behaviour: "If nothing bad happened last time, do what I did last time."

The evolutionary basis for this default behaviour does not need much explanation. In risk-averse modes (all mail order has an element of uncertainty and risk) it is sensible to be conservative. This conservatism applies to our taste in food: we feel very comfortable eating food which tastes identical to food we have eaten in the past, since the very fact that we are contemplating the decision is evidence that it did not kill us in the past. Ray Kroc, the former owner of McDonald's, spotted this tendency: "People don't want the best burger in the world," he stated, "they want one which tastes just like the one they had last time."

In a desktop internet scenario the force of habit is strengthened by a significant factor. First of all there are none of the other confounding factors (such as proximity or happenstance) that nudge us out of our well-trodden paths. But there is also a further boost to the "familiarity breeds contentment" in online shopping: the cognitive burden of using any unfamiliar website is really quite high. A site you have used 20 times in the last year can be used with a degree of unconscious fluency -- whereas a new site requires painful, conscious mental effort, generating uncertainty and doubt. (Think of the first few kilometres you drive in a hire car, where all the controls are in a different place to the car you own at home -- or the bemusement you experience in a traditional shop when they rearrange the shelving.)

Again, habit amplifies the abundance of the Matthew Effect. The more often that people go to your site, the more likely they are to come back.

The other default by which we live all the time is "do what everyone else does". Economists choose to ignore this behaviour, or deride it as "irrational" for a rather self-serving reason: once it is accepted that one person's behaviour may affect that of another, it makes a horrendous mess of their orderly mathematical models. But we would not be recognisably human at all had we not developed the sensible instinct of copying the behaviour of others. Given limited time and energy, to go with the flow of mass behaviour is both necessary for survival (your tribe can either all fight or all run away -- both are preferable to half of you doing one thing, half the other), and cognitively efficient (it draws on collective knowledge and experience, rather than individual enquiry, and allows learned behaviour to spread much faster).

Why do businesses and governments make such egregious errors in understanding customer and citizen behavior? Because they are unaware of them. Why? Because, frankly, we are largely unaware of them ourselves.

In understanding customer behaviour, companies have traditionally used two tools to determine likely purchasing intent. One is the standard assumptions of neoclassical economic theory, which is psychologically blind: the kind of "perfect" transactions it models are almost never found in reality. In the economist's mind, people are calculating rationalists, merely seeking to maximise their own utility in a world of perfect information, and devoid of such concepts as uncertainty, mistrust, fear and regret. Yet the human is far less a rational calculating machine than a kind of anxious, moralising, herd-like, reciprocating, image-conscious, story-telling game theorist.

The other tool most widely used in ascertaining and predicting consumer preference is market research. This, in truth, is little better than the economic model, as we don't really know why we do what we do. We're good at pretending to know, or constructing plausible-sounding post-rationalisations of our behaviour. But the heuristics that influence and, at times, determine our actions operate on us at a purely unconscious level. Hence research cannot really uncover much in the way of explanation for people's behaviour, since the people you are researching often do not understand why they behave as they do. Moreover, when in groups, the explanations people contrive may be more motivated by the urge to impress the strangers in the room than to give the researcher any true insights. (It isn't only companies which have marketing departments -- the brain has a pretty active marketing function of its own.)

So what I am saying here is that both the standard tools we use to predict and model human behaviour are really quite bad. Our ability to model and predict may therefore be little better than, say, weather forecasting in the 1820s. Now this is the critical question. We shall, I suspect, never be able to predict human behaviour exactly -- any more that we can ever issue a perfect weather forecast for next year. But what if we could just develop models that improved it by just a bit? We are, after all, starting from a low base...

Much as we all love to decry it, weather forecasting has improved markedly. A four-day forecast today is as accurate as a two-day forecast in 1985. The path of a hurricane can be predicted now within a course over 65 percent narrower than 40 years ago. More important perhaps, weather forecasting has improved in another way too -- it now acknowledges the limits to its powers. It has learned that the ability to forecast anything more than ten days ahead may be computationally impossible. Knowing the limits to your understanding is a form of intellectual progress in itself.

What if economics and market research were to achieve a similar leap forward both in its ability to predict and in its understanding of its limitations? What would the implications be for business and government efficiency and for economic growth and well being?

Books such as Nudge and Thinking, Fast and Slow have topped the bestseller lists. "Big data" now provides real-time behavioural information that will make it easier to test smaller behavioural experiments. Computer modelling -- the very technology that has transformed weather forecasting -- better depicts the complexity of actual market behaviour than the naïve Newtonian models of conventional economics. Darwinian psychology provides insights into those parts of our instinctive nature that we can change -- and those we can't. And I haven't even mentioned neuroscience. Will these ever provide us with a perfect means to predict and adjust human tastes and actions? Not a chance.

On the other hand, how much would our understanding need to improve before we would notice a significant improvement in economic effects, in quality of life -- and in the intelligence of political debate? Remember, we are starting from a very low base -- where intelligent people can be diametrically wrong in their predictions of the likely shape of online retail.

If the success of new product launches were to grow from the current six percent to ten, how much more could profitably be spent on R&D? Is it from psychological progress, not from physical technology, that we should expect the greater parts of the next 20 years?

I hold out rather small hopes for the gains for further scientific innovation. Once you've progressed from horsepower to the Boeing 747, it is far harder to enjoy a similar increase in velocity again. But what if the next century were marked as the golden age of progress in social sciences? That seems far more feasible and desirable.

Or, as the great Robert Trivers puts it: "In short, Darwinian social theory gives us a glimpse of an underlying symmetry and logic in social relationships which, when more fully comprehended by ourselves, should revitalise our political understanding and provide the intellectual support for a science and medicine of psychology. In the process it should also give us a deeper understanding of the many roots of our suffering."

About Rory Sutherland

Rory Sutherland is the Executive Creative Director at Ogilvy One and Vice-Chairman of Ogilvy and Mather UK, rising from his first position there in 1988 as a junior copywriter. Rory stands at the center of an advertising revolution in brand identities, designing cutting-edge, interactive campaigns that blur the line between ad and entertainment.

Learn more about Rory Sutherland by following him on Twitter @rorysutherland

Chapter 19:

Knowledge Is The New Land

by Joe Green, president and co-founder, FWD.us

The arc of human economic history, in broad brush-strokes, runs from hunter-gathering, to agriculture, to the industrial economy. We are now entering a new phase: the knowledge economy.

Europeans first came to the Americas because land was plentiful and well-suited for agriculture. In Europe most people were tenant farmers, and there was little chance for life to get better. In America, you could own land and be a yeoman farmer: the first middle class. Then we had our first great economic transformation into an industrial economy. This created great wealth, great advances in life expectancy, and great geographic disruption as people moved from farms to cities – pollution and massive inequality followed. As a response to these issues in the United States, we saw the first real growth in the social sector of legislation – free public education, child labor laws, the income tax, and the minimum wage.

What we're currently experiencing in the tech industry is representative of a major shift from an industrial to a knowledge economy. The two major facets that are changing are globalization and technology. Globalization creates a global market for both product and labor. Technology allows for innovation and development to happen anywhere, more and more, but it also allows increasingly greater automation and greater productivity. In a factory, only a certain number of widgets can be made each hour. But one software engineer can be almost unlimitedly productive, and his or her market can grow globally because he or she can create a product and make it available to the world. And that's where technology and globalization intersect.

In a world that is both globalized and knowledge-based, it pays to be an immigrant nation. Diversity of ideas, opinions and backgrounds provide the perfect fuel for a knowledge economy. America is an immigrant nation, where the exchange of ideas and the diversity of opinions can thrive; this also holds true in other immigrant nations such as Brazil and Israel. My ancestors came to America from small villages in Eastern Europe, but they were willing to pick up their things and embark on a ship for a month and go to a country they'd never even seen a picture of. What makes us an entrepreneurial country is a product of the courage and openness and grit it takes to go on that immigrant journey.

Supporting entrepreneurial countries and, in turn, the knowledge economy, means investing in people. If in the industrial era the inputs were land, labor, machines, and natural resources, the inputs in a knowledge economy are people: that's why you see really successful tech companies pumping so much investment into human resources and employee benefits. But we can't afford for this investment to just happen at a corporate level. Governments need to understand, too, that the way we work and innovate has completely changed and that this change is ongoing. To keep up, governments need to redouble their investment in people. Driving policy for a digitally connected world fueled by knowledge is about a lot more than the obvious (and important) hot-button issues like broadband regulation and intellectual property concerns. Equally important are the decisions we make about our education system, scientific research, and our immigration policies.

Even in a globalized, virtually connected world, physical proximity to colleagues and other innovators remains highly important. That's why, on a micro level, we've seen a boom in co-working spaces for independent workers, and why, on a macro level, we see cities like New York and San Francisco and London becoming centers of knowledge and diversity that may have more in common with one another than they do with the towns next door. This will only going to become more important on a global policy level if we are going to thrive both culturally and economically. How do we fix our legal immigration system? How do we bring the people outside of these thriving knowledge hubs into the knowledge economy, to promote a culture of inclusion and diversity, not polarization?

Nations that tackle these issues head-on will not only produce the most innovative companies and ideas, but will also secure their place in a future economy fueled by people. This is a test we will face in the coming years, and I believe we will pass.

Joe Green, President: FWD.us

Joe Green, founded FWD.us to organize and engage the tech community on issues of vital importance to America's global competitiveness. Previously, he founded Causes and co-founded NationBuilder to realize his belief that social networks enable community organizing at a previously unknown scale.

Learn more about Joe Green at www.fwd.us

Chapter 20:

The Collaborative Economy

Robin Chase, founder, Zipcar/Buzzcar; in conversation with Lisa Gansky, founder, Mesh Labs

LISA GANSKY: I'm curious what you're thinking in terms of, first of all, the whole lexicon problem of the "sharing," "collaborative," "mesh," "peer," "informal" economy stuff. Are you landing on any particular place about all the language? Are people getting less confused?

ROBIN CHASE: I like to think that we are moving away from a capitalist, industrial economy to something new, and that something new will certainly be larger than the "sharing economy." When most people think about the word "sharing," as I see it, they're thinking person-to-person and hard assets.

I like to think of this new economy that we're moving to and what we're seeing in terms of what technology is enabling as much broader than that. It's not just person-to-person or peer-to-peer, it's person-to-business, peer-to-government, government-to-peer -- and it's not just about assets, it's about sharing our expertise, our networks, excess capacity and how we can tap into it. I do like this term "collaborative economy." Or, as I've talked about with Seth Godin before, "connection economy."

LG: I think we're converging on using "the collaborative economy" as a general phrase that applies to peer-to-peer networks and marketplaces but can also address tools libraries and community kitchens and gardens and corporations sharing IP, 3D printing, advanced manufacturing, the maker movement, crowdsourcing and crowdfunding and hopefully a whole host of things that haven't even made their appearance yet. I think we're in the middle of recasting a social operating system, just like for computers we've been living in the industrial operating system and now we're creating a new "Social Operating System." The impact of that is phenomenal and exciting and, like a computer operating system, calls all it touches into question. We now have the first stages of the marketplaces, practices and systems that are emerging from that shift and, I'm also feeling very optimistic that more and more corporations, governments and individuals are entering into the conversation with more enthusiasm and openness and less fear and denial.

RC: The emphasis is on this idea of collaboration. In the industrial economy, the model was closed, proprietary systems, and one entity did an entire vertical stack and the company did it all itself. Technology has opened up the possibilities by reducing transaction costs and making finding, aggregating, sorting, and dealing with other entities simple. The future lies in collaboration where each entity, whether they are an individual or a company or a government, really is focused on doing the aspect of work or service that they themselves do best. What I think you and I have discovered is that when you think about peers or small companies, there are some things that they innately do much better. It's all about collaboration.

LG: Riffing off of what you were just saying, in the "old economy," the industrial model was organized around the emphasis on ownership and control of, in the case of businesses, whole value chains. Like Kodak, I've joked that they owned the cows to make the bones to make the agar to make the film that no one buys. You end up with these really tight, highly verticalized value chains and the control and barriers to entry that really come from a military model – we've all but moved away from that. Instead of one-to-many, it's many-to-many. Look at GE. It's been impressive to me how much crowdsourcing they've been doing and it's actually now starting to positively impact their core business. Take a look at their home page. It's 2 young guys talking about 3D printing! Increasingly I think companies and governments are taking the point of view that innovation is not going to come from within the enterprise. It's going to come from,…who knows where. So how do you create the friendly front door, the trust/Brand/relationships or API, to welcome innovators who don't know you or trust you but could be the key to solving your industry's future challenges?

RC: As you talked about, and as we both agree, I look at company and government and they do have these things that they are particularly good at, which is spending a lot of money to make complex things simple. And if they do it right, they take what they have learned and what they are good at and they open it up for engagement by people who have things to offer that big companies don't. If we think about innovation specifically, what we know is that many minds produce vastly more innovation and creativity than any discrete number of brains thinking about a problem. The whole open data movement and Innocentive and Quirky -- they've done this, they've built a platform for participation, which I think companies do well, and they're going to open up and make those standards open to individuals who can now input the things that they do well.

These institutions are very high-growth, scalable, resource-efficient and also are -- to a certain extent -- more humane because we are recognizing the value of individual contributions.

LG: I think you said something that's really important there -- in a way, when new movements come in there's this four-stage cycle that's usually first ignore, then chuckle, then be afraid, then accept. We're moving through these stages really fast now as opposed to what I remember from when we went through the initial introduction of the Internet into commerce. You commented on something that I think has evoked a lot of fear, which is how do people get credit or where is the currency or value exchange. As we move from a model where there's clear ownership and there's a clear transaction, to something that's more a commons or collaborative approach, have you seen people be concerned about compensation, meaningful value capture, or feeling like they're contributing and trying to track that aspect?

RC: Well, there's a lot I want to say about that. I think there's actually a fifth stage to that process you mentioned. If we're looking at the Internet right now, it has captured by the biggest entities. Where we really want to end up is a future state of equilibrium and mutual standoff of the small and nimble versus the big and strong. Where we don't want to end up in the collaborative economy is big companies figuring this out and therefore capturing it and owning it all. The solution for me, is to move it beyond the acceptance and the capture to an equilibrium of both sides having power. We need to make sure that we continue to give power out to the individuals who are contributing. I think some transactions will be monetized and some will not, and I don't have the answers for whether our new economy will be fully money-based or whether some of our currency will be in the form of intangibles that still provide real value.

LG: It's interesting. The whole idea of "capture," as you call it, is basically saying that the collaborative economy will be like the Borg -- resistance is futile, you must be assimilated -- and that capitalism will still thrive in the old model of what we currently have. The idea that corporations could own the collaborative economy is sort of fundamentally missing the opportunity of a social operating system shift or ontological shift where ownership in that way will also be transformed. The emergence of the Benefit Corporation legal distinction shines a light in the direction I favor it going. It all needs to be 'social enterprise'.

RC: This collaboration economy is largely organized through platforms and standards. Some of those platforms that organize the collaboration economy are distributed and owned by no one. I would say that the Internet once was that, and now it's being captured and controlled by some large technology companies and telcos. I think we're going to see two types of platforms -- those owned by companies, like Airbnb and Google. When a platform gets big it becomes so large that it becomes a monopoly, and that monopoly power tends to not care about those that are contributing. This is what we have to combat, and why those companies need to pro-actively figure out how to give power back to individual contributors.

LG: I think that what we're struggling with right now as a global economy is that value creation and value capture are misaligned and that what we are hoping will happen as a function of a lot of these models -- some of these "collaborative economy" companies will go public, but many of the people who have been fueling their growth aren't *owners* in terms of equity in the company. The lion's share of the capital will be captured by the one-percent, the venture capitalists and a few founders. I'm challenging people to create these companies in a cooperative model where the people offering goods and services participate in the health and wealth of their platform.

RC: Having tried to build many platforms, I know that they cost a huge amount of money. There are some successes of platforms built by individuals-- look at Wikipedia. But more typically it will be the private sector that builds these. The government can do this as well: GPS was funded by the government to do its own military things, and they opened it up and now it's a public good.

LG: A lot of the technologies that underlie infrastructure-related things, and GPS is a good example. Also health and transportation data, the opening up of the data and sharing it liberally across departments, cities, communities, private-public, have had enormous benefits which we are just beginning to see. Code For America has proven to be a perfect platform to create engagement and impact. We've seen the birth of the urban entrepreneur, people like you who have created solutions to major challenges in cities.

RC: When I'm advising governments and companies, I keep telling them, open as much stuff as you can so that we can get all this innovation out and so that entrepreneurs have some great free or very-low-cost inputs that they wouldn't otherwise have. That's how we can keep things moving.

Robin Chase, Founder and CEO: Buzzcar

Robin Chase is founder and CEO of Buzzcar, a service that brings together car owners and drivers in a carsharing marketplace. Formerly founder and CEO of Zipcar, Robin has dedicated her career to minimizing humanity's negative impact on the environment by opening channels for sharing.

Learn more about Robin Chase at www.robinchase.org

Lisa Gansky, Founder: Mesh Labs

Lisa Gansky is an entrepreneur, investor, speaker and author of the bestselling book, The Mesh: Why the Future of Business is Sharing and the chief instigator of Mesh Labs. She works in the design of new products, policies, services, partnerships and models in which 'access' to goods, services and talent triumphs over the ownership of them.

Learn more about Lisa Gansky at www.lisagansky.com

A Summary

by Caroline McCarthy, "On: The Future Of Now" editor

"This isn't about marketing." That's probably the most common phrase that came out of my mouth (or across my keyboard) when I was communicating with the incredible array of contributors to this book. I didn't want jargon about eyeballs or monetization, I didn't want essay after essay drooling over brilliant brand campaigns or mockery of the #suxorz and #fails, and I wanted to keep use of the word "disrupt" to small and tasteful quantities. I'm a marketer by trade -- for a fantastic advertising company, true[x] Media -- and so perhaps I was a little oversensitive about letting my day job percolate too much into this project.

But I'm glad that we were diligent, with curators Toby and Craig's full support. This book instead turned into a collection of deeply personal takes on everything from the value of art to what Westerners can learn from emerging markets to the problems with how we talk about sex online. And I think that's really emblematic of "the future of now." Social media and connectivity have crept into every corner of our lives, and no longer can a single industry, region, or demographic claim to own the conversation on it. As we move forward, with social and mobile technologies taking on bigger and more quotidian roles in everyone's lives (and, somewhat paradoxically, fading into the background and normalcy of our lives as they grow ever more important) it's increasingly crucial that all backgrounds, cultures, and perspectives are represented here. Social Media Week and Nokia have worked hard to curate a vision that encompasses all this.

I was also thrilled to be able to truly incorporate the individual voices of all our contributors, from academics to entrepreneurs to artists. I made a few additions, sure, but most of them were just Oxford commas.

Acknowledgements

To everyone that has helped to make the book happen -- the people that have supported me over the years, including my mentor Andrew Rasiej who always asked me the toughest questions, and to all my advisors, friends and collaborators. Thank you to Craig Hepburn and all the amazing people at Nokia, our local Social Media Week partners, and of course my team, especially my rocks Brian Leddy, Zach Smith, Nicky Yates, and Ben Scheim. Thanks to Caroline McCarthy who worked tirelessly to secure such an incredible array of people to contribute to the book and for her dedication and diligence in transcribing, re-writing and editing every chapter. And to each of our amazing contributors. Without your inspired words this book would literally just be a preface and a book cover. Not only will sharing your contributions inspire thousands of people, but your support will also help people in the developing world access clean and safe drinking water for the first time through our nonprofit partner charity:water.

Finally, I want to thank my beautiful, amazing wife who has literally been by my side since week one of Social Media Week, I love you and I am eternally grateful for your unwavering support.

Here's to the next iteration.

- Toby

I want to thank Toby Daniels for his collaboration on this book and his whole team at Crowdcentric for being amazing partners to work with and long may that continue. Year on year our teams have worked so hard to ensure that Social Media Week has been a huge success in every city that's hosted the event and enabled Nokia to develop stronger relationships with our consumers and advocates across the world. For that i would also like to thank my whole team at Nokia for being rockstars and the Nokia leadership team for supporting and believing in our joint vision in Social Media Week.

And to my incredible wife and best friend Jane who puts up with far more than she should but constantly inspires me and keeps me on track in life! To our two beautiful wee legends Connor & Arran i love you all very much. You guys mean the world to me.

- Craig

About Social Media Week

Social Media Week, a leading media platform and worldwide event with the mission of capturing, curating and sharing the most meaningful ideas, trends, and best practices with regard to technology and social media's impact on business, society and culture.

About Crowdcentric Media

Crowdcentric Media wants to help make a future where technology and humanity come together to create a more open, connected and sustainable world. We help businesses thrive at the intersection of media, technology and communication.

About the Curators

Toby Daniels

Toby is the co-founder and CEO Crowdcentric and founder and Executive Director of Social Media Week. Through his work with Crowdcentric Toby wants to design a future where technology and humanity come together to create a more open, connected and sustainable world.

Toby has been featured extensively in mainstream and trade media, including articles on CNN.com, The NY Times, The Next Web, Huffington Post, BBC, PSFK and Fast Company. He speaks regularly at conferences and has given talks at PdF Latin America in Santiago Chile, Social Media Brazil in São Paulo, PDMA's Co-Creation Conference, Phoenix, SXSW, Austin, V2V, Las Vegas and Social Media Week in Bogota, Mumbai, London, LA, Chicago and New York.

In addition to his professional endeavors, Toby is also a passionate contributor to a number of non-profit organizations, including CampInteractive (CI), for which he has served as a senior board member for 7 years, and charity:water, which he has been working closely with and supporting since 2009.

Toby is also a founding board chair of PVBLIC Foundation, an in-kind grant-making organization that harnesses the power of unused media assets to drive social change.

Craig Hepburn

Craig is Global Director of Digital & Social Media at Nokia, responsible for leading a world class digital and social media team. Over the past 4 years Nokia's social and digital media standards where success has improved so much that they are now globally recognized as one of the most forward thinking and successful brands using social and digital marketing.

Craig has a very strong background in Enterprise Content Management strategies, digital marketing and user experience design and who joined Nokia from Open Text where as Director of Social Media Strategy he advised and consulted on social media and Enterprise 2.0 strategies for some of the worlds largest brands.

Previously, he headed up the global eCommerce and digital marketing strategy for STA Travel and is credited with delivering cutting edge technologies to enhance the online travel agency's hugely successful online presence and web strategy.

Craig was voted as one of the UK's rising stars in the digital marketing sector by Revolution Magazine, shortlisted for digital person of the year by the DADI awards and contributes to many publications on social media and digital marketing.

-

Caroline McCarthy

Caroline is a former print and television journalist, an ex-Googler, a book and blog editor, and now the vice president of communications and content at true[x] Media, an advertising startup headquartered in Los Angeles and New York.